English Span

Coloring Book for Kids

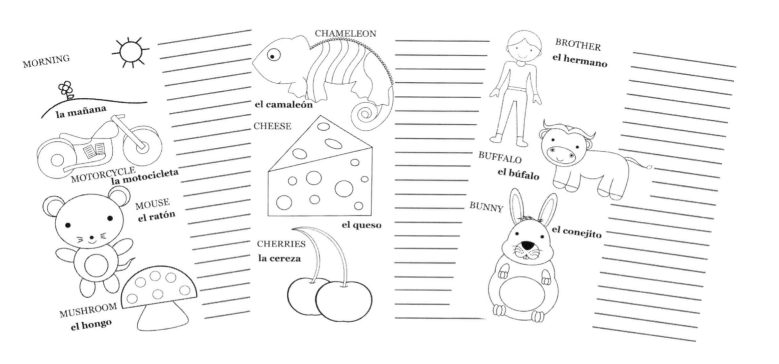

ISBN-13: 978-1985030688

ISBN-10: 1985030683

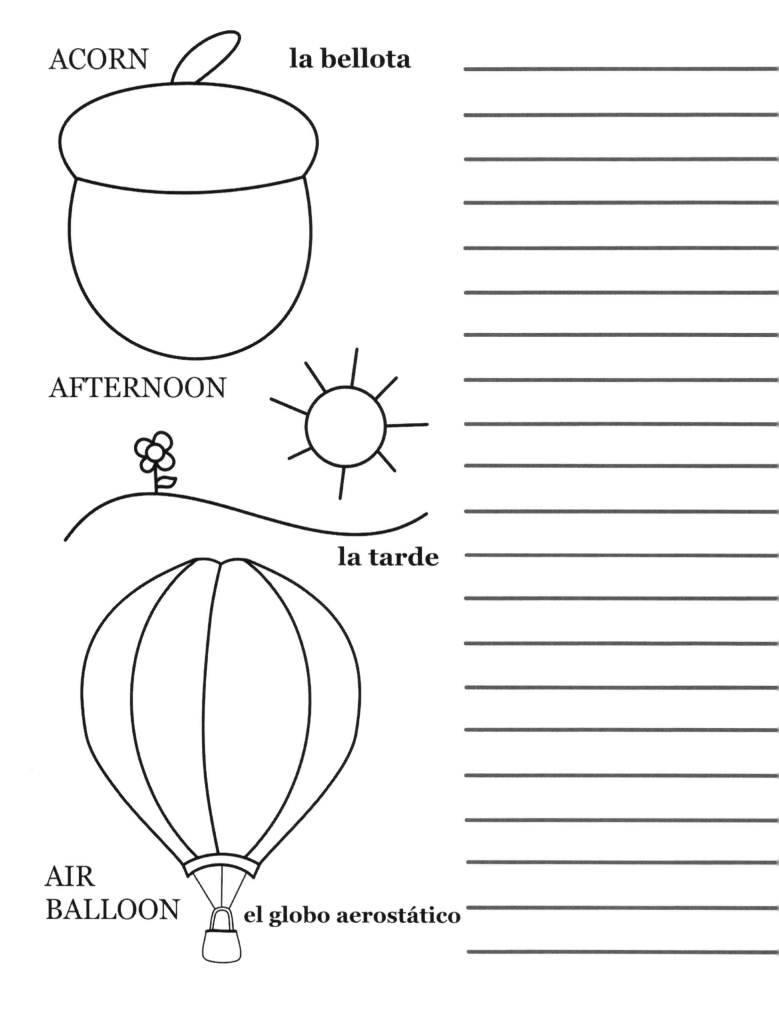

ACORN **la bellota**

AFTERNOON

la tarde

AIR
BALLOON **el globo aerostático**

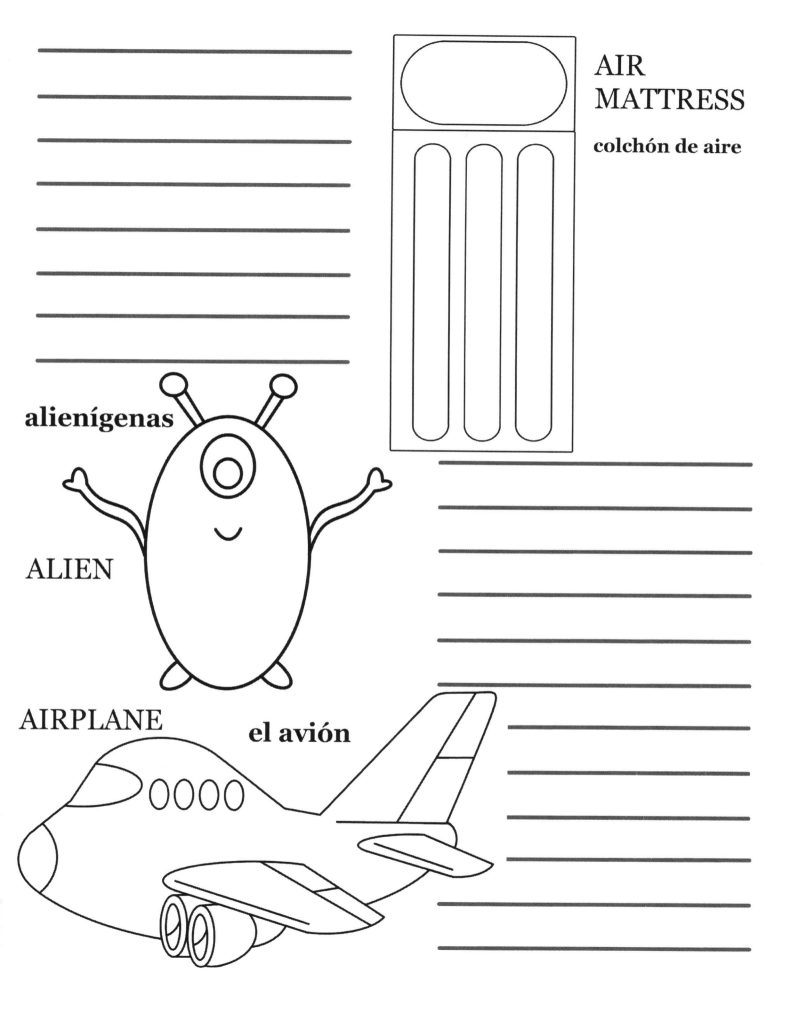

AIR
MATTRESS

colchón de aire

alienígenas

ALIEN

AIRPLANE el avión

ALLIGATOR

el caimán

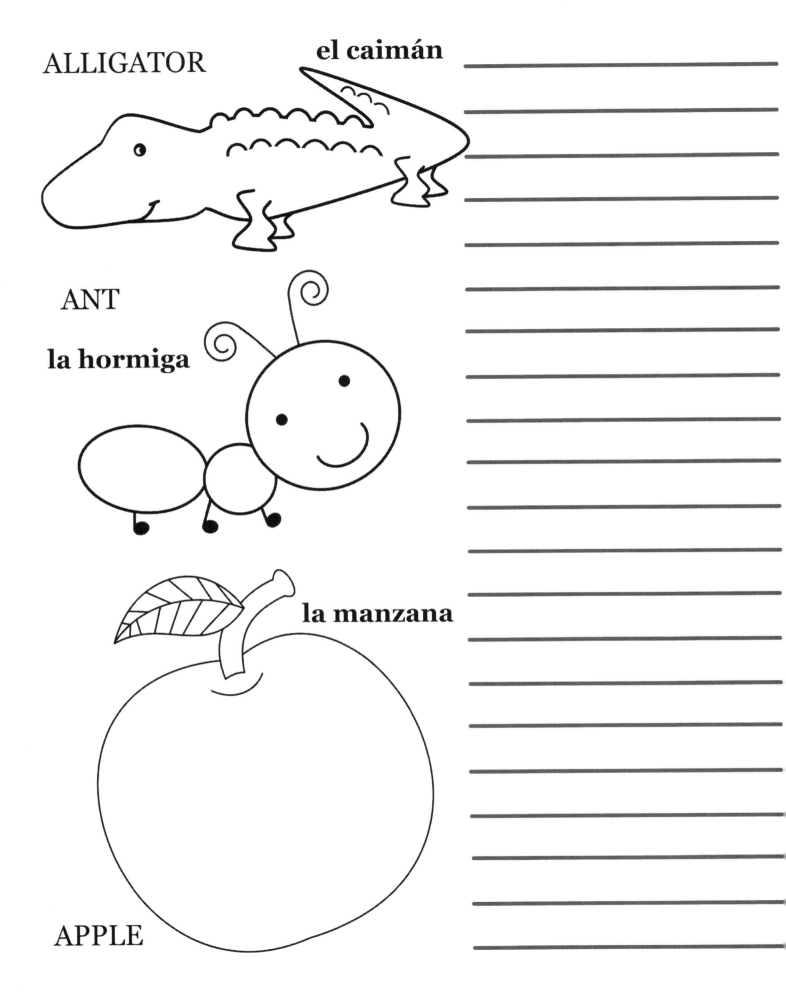

ANT

la hormiga

la manzana

APPLE

APRON **el delantal**

ARMADILLO **el armadillo**

ARTIST PALETTE

paleta del artista

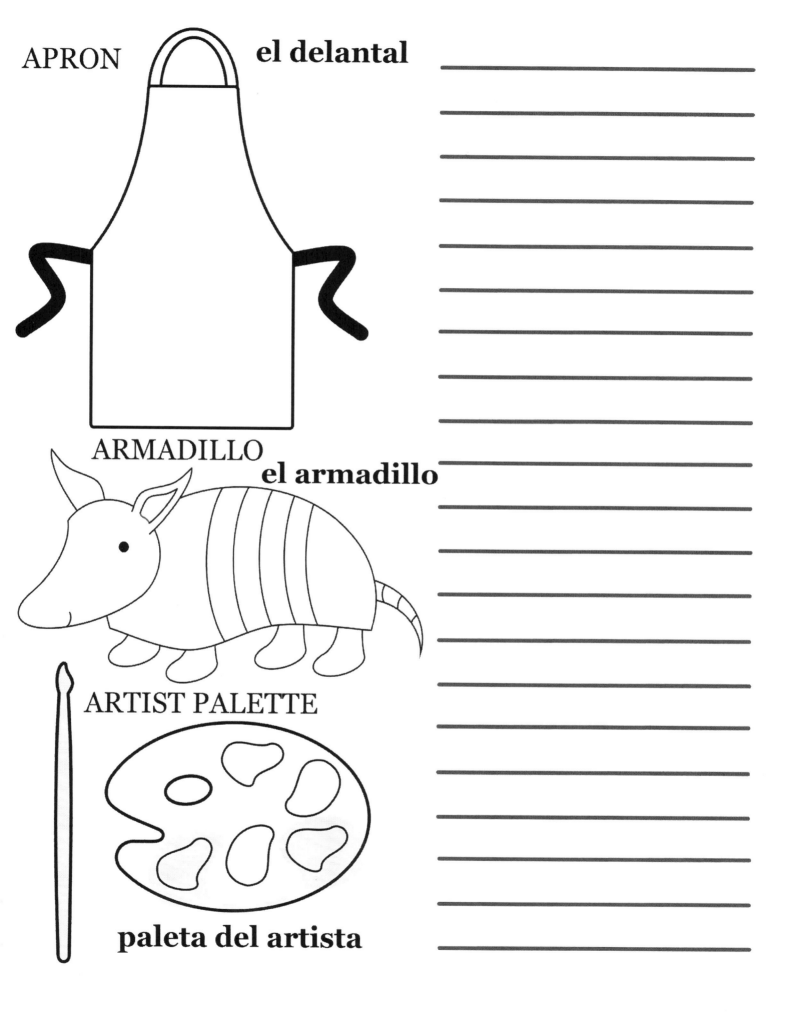

ASTRONAUT

astronauta

BABY BOTTLE

la mamadera

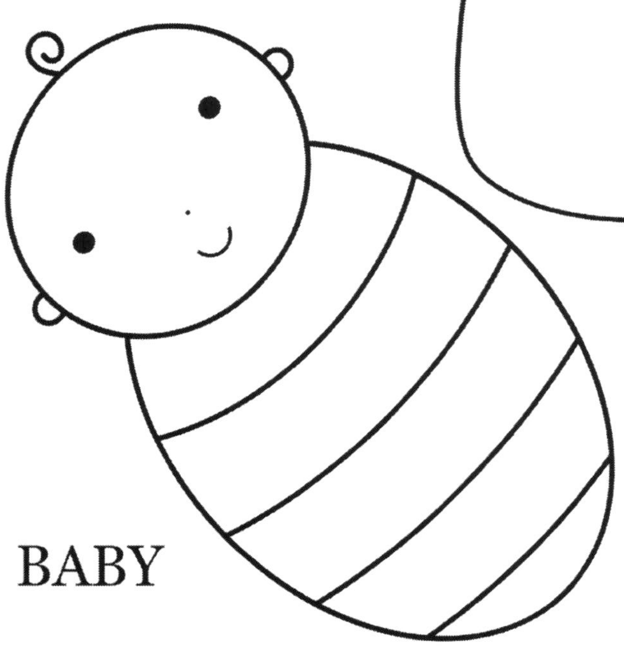

bebé

BABY

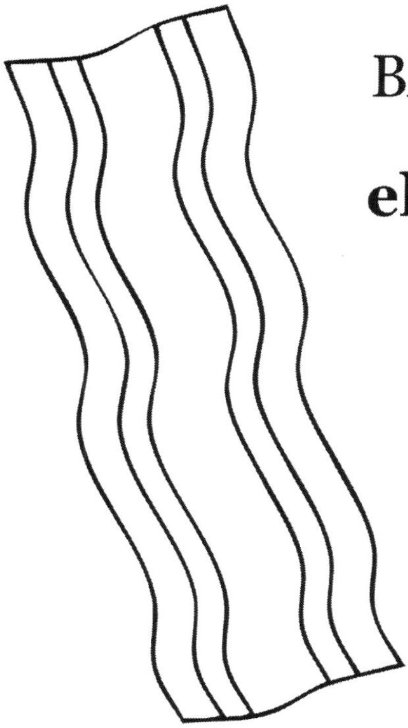

BACON

el tocino

BADMINGTON

el bádminton

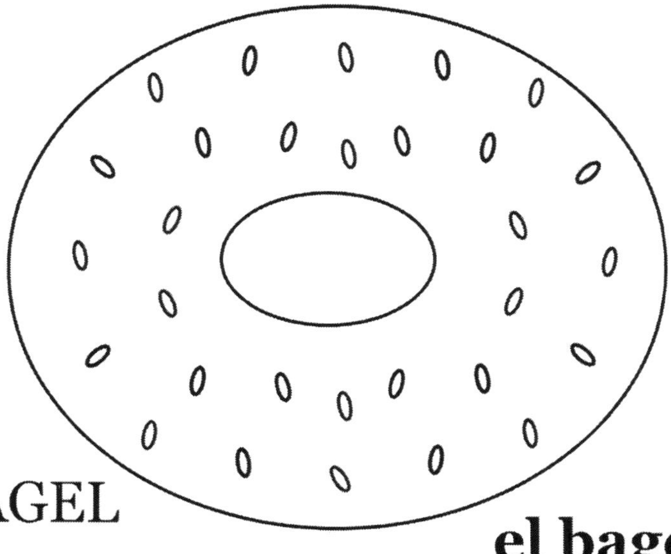

BAGEL

el bagel

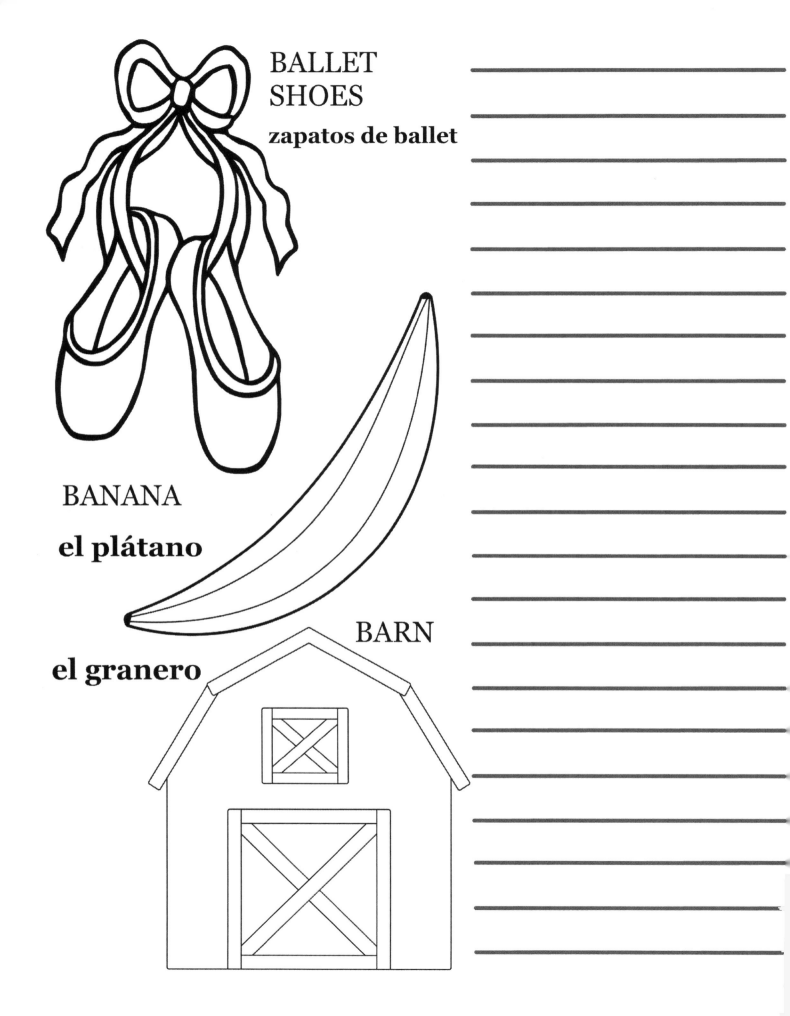

BALLET
SHOES

zapatos de ballet

BANANA

el plátano

BARN

el granero

BASEBALL **el béisbol**

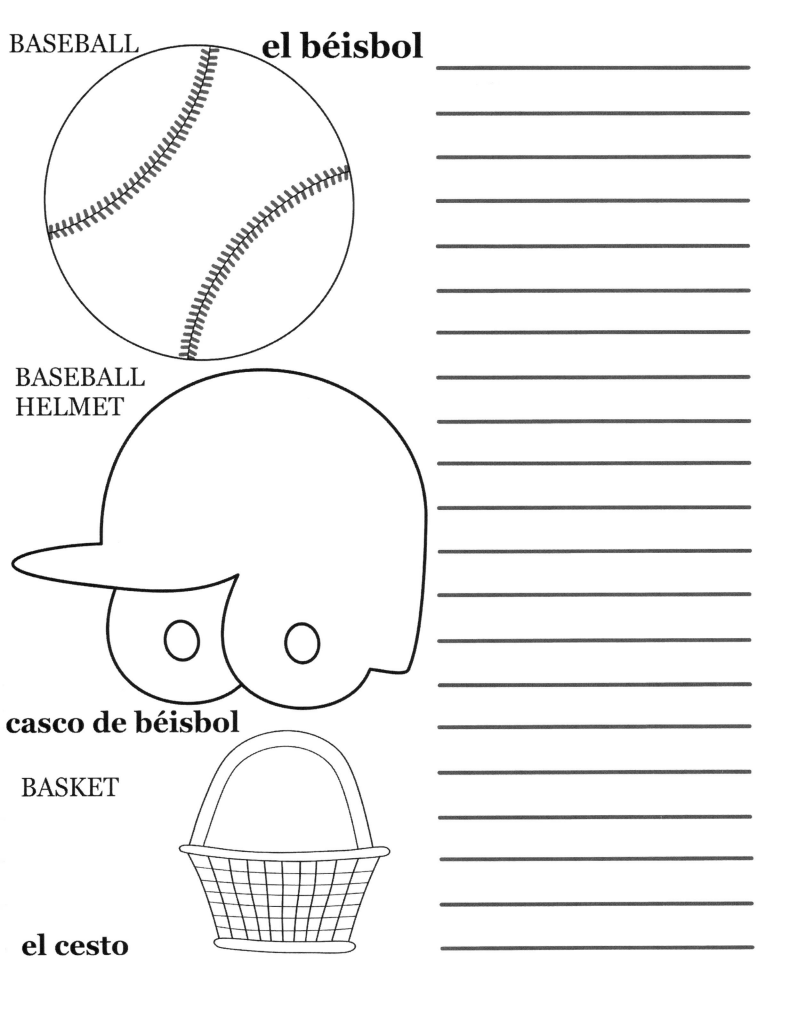

BASEBALL
HELMET

casco de béisbol

BASKET

el cesto

BASKETBALL

el baloncesto

el murciélago

BAT

BATHTUB

la bañera

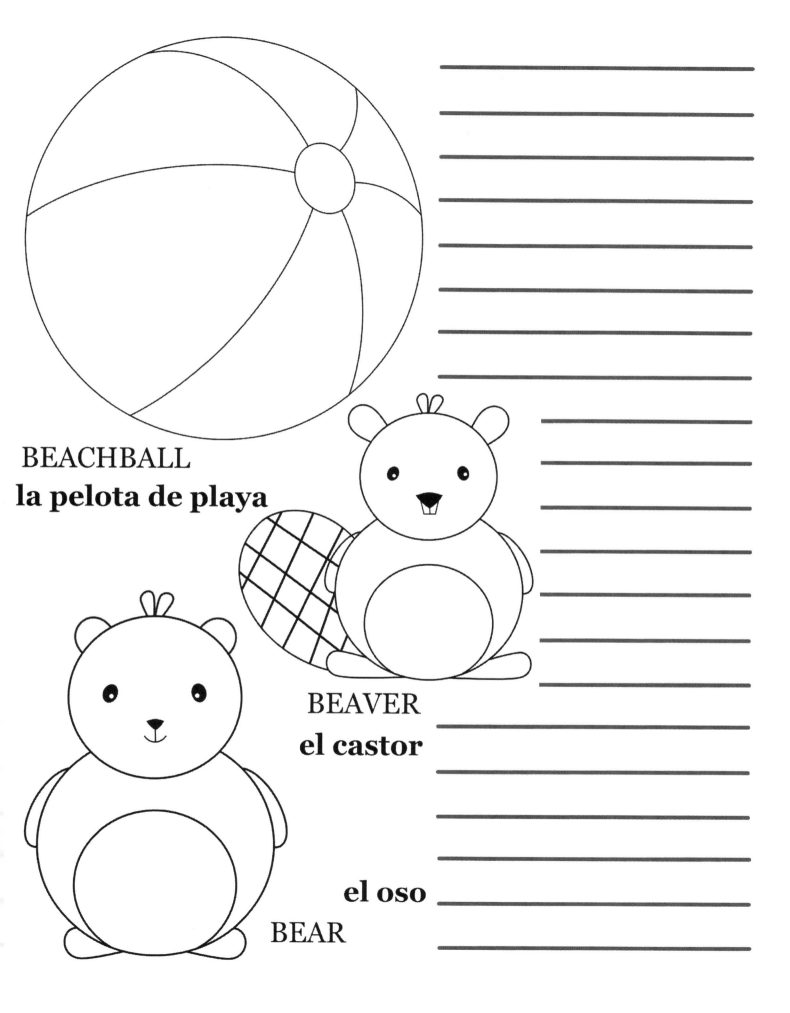

BEACHBALL
la pelota de playa

BEAVER
el castor

el oso
BEAR

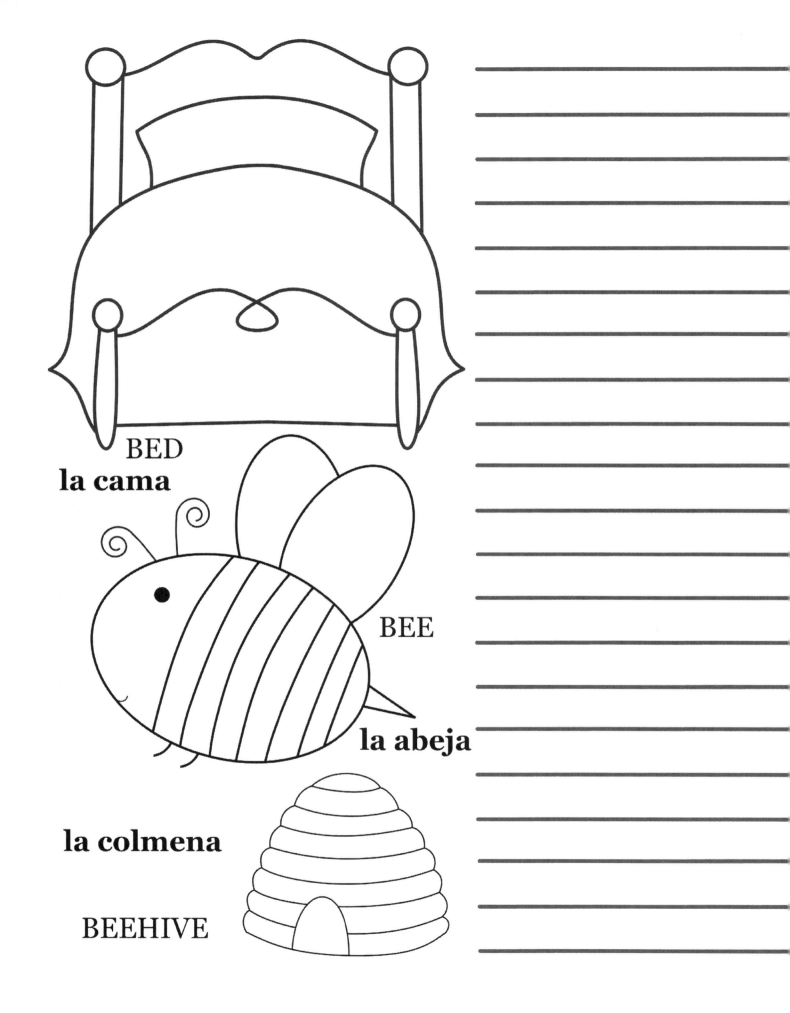

BED

la cama

BEE

la abeja

la colmena

BEEHIVE

BEET

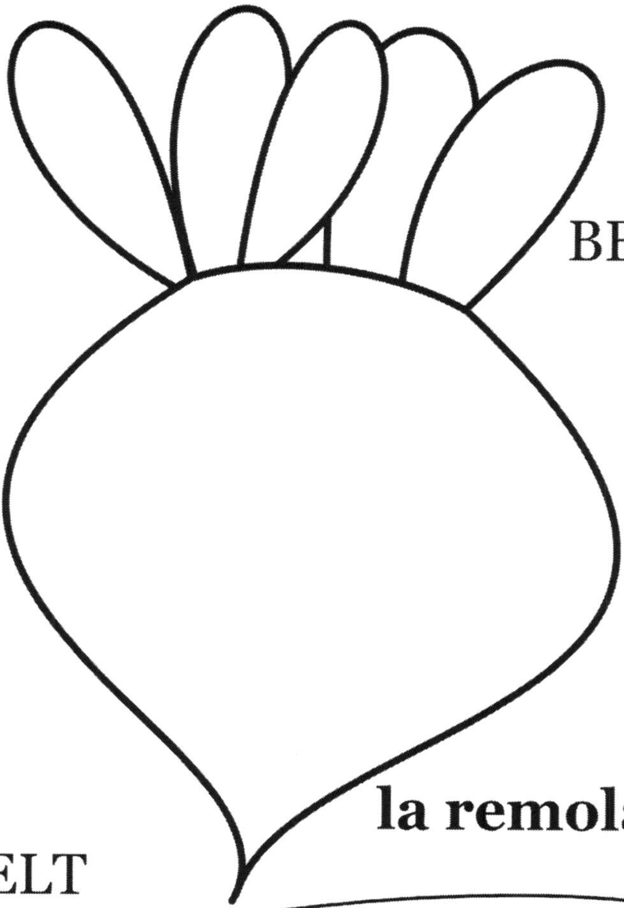

la remolacha

BELT

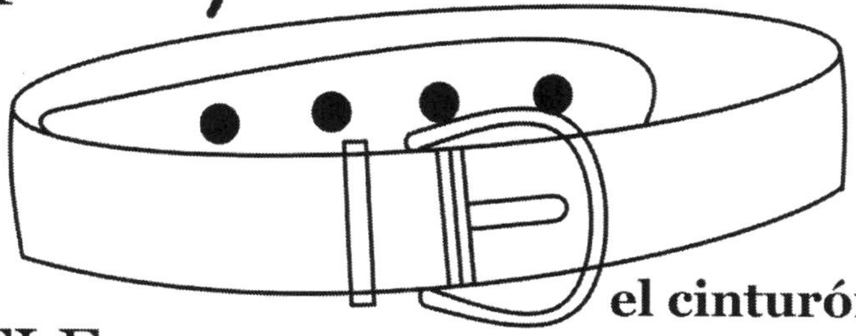

el cinturón

BEETLE

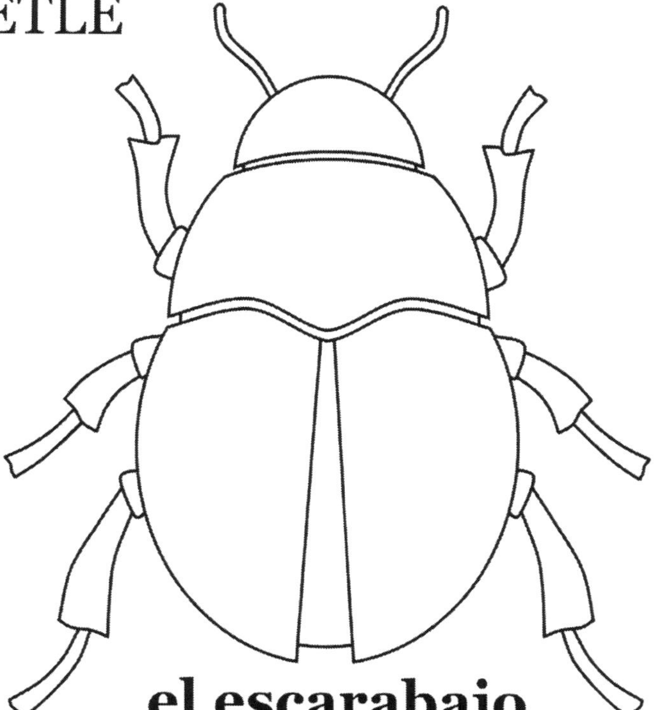

el escarabajo

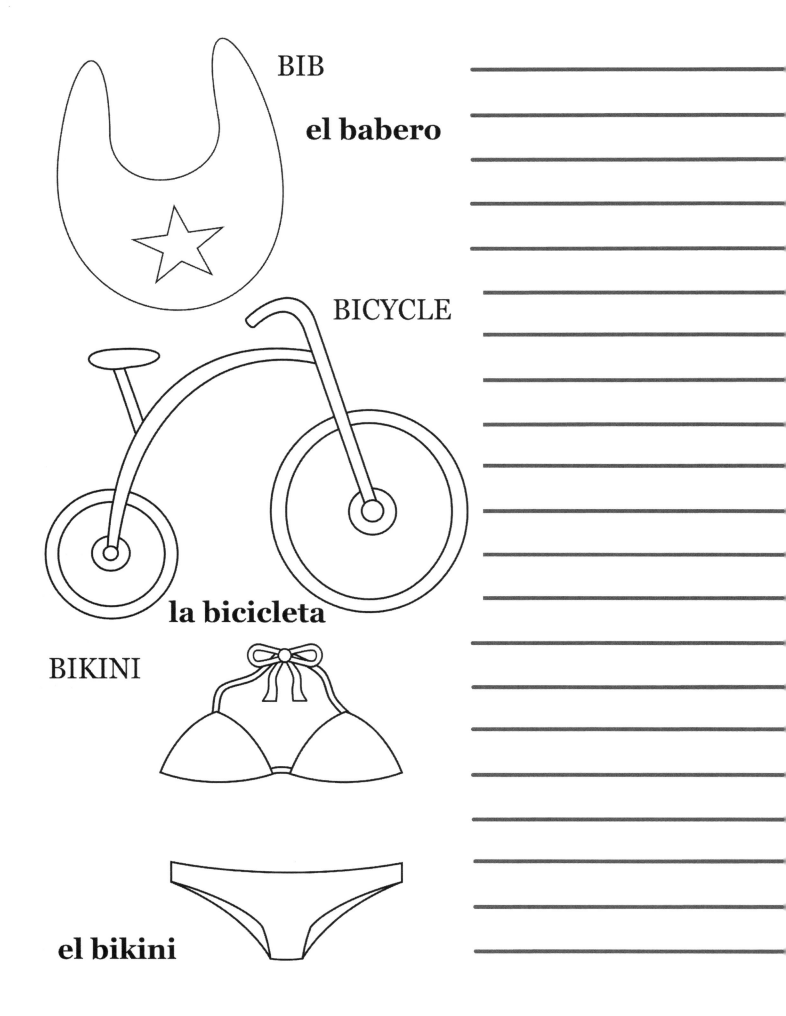

BIB

el babero

BICYCLE

la bicicleta

BIKINI

el bikini

BINOCULARS

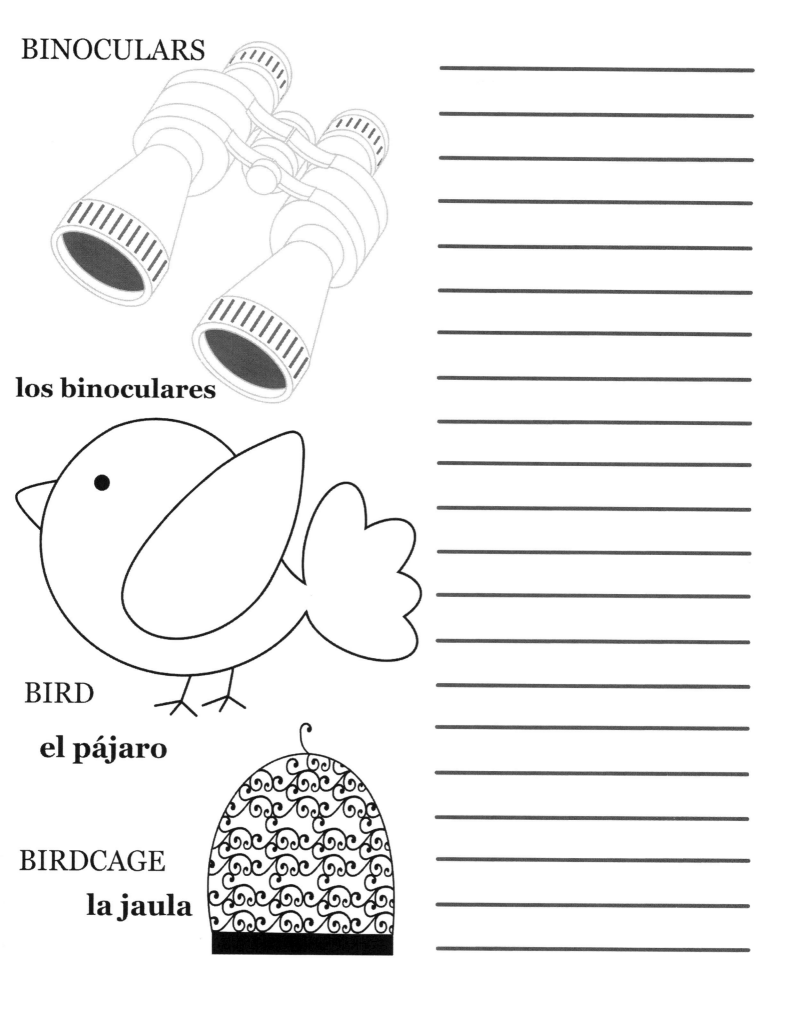

los binoculares

BIRD

el pájaro

BIRDCAGE

la jaula

BOAT

el barco

BOOK

el libro

BOW

el lazo

BOWL

el cuenco

BOWLING

los bolos

BREAD

el pan

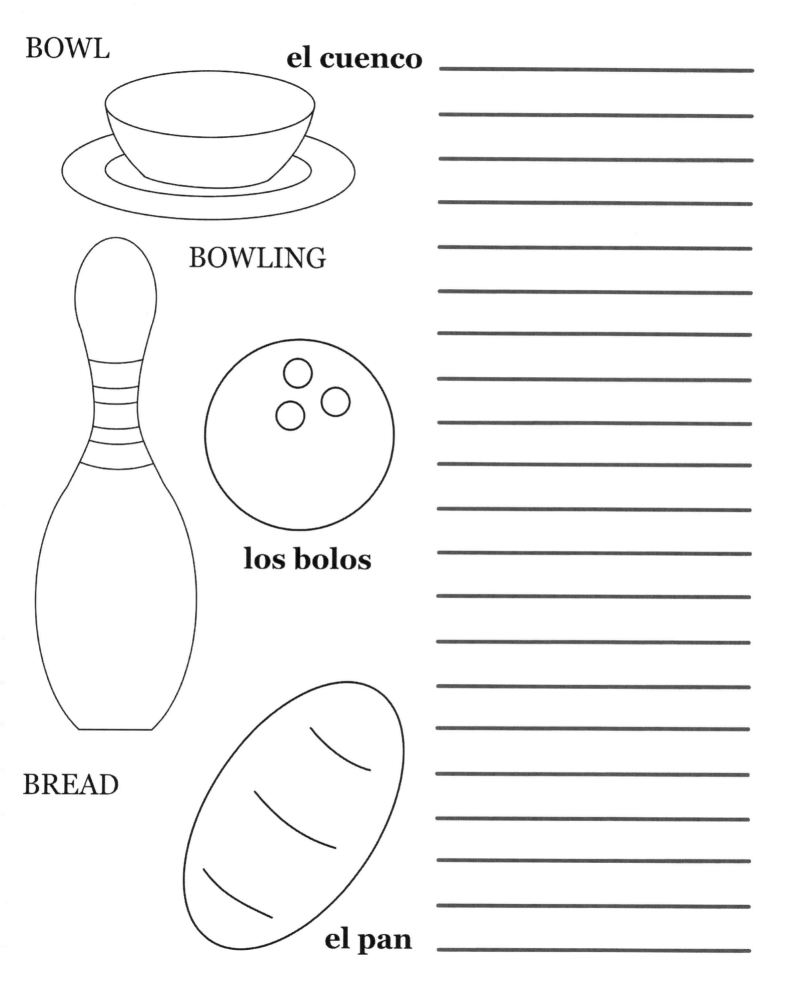

BROTHER
el hermano

BUFFALO
el búfalo

BUNNY
el conejito

BUS
el autobús

BUTTERFLY
la mariposa

CAKE

el pastel

CALCULATOR

la calculadora

CAMEL

el camello

CAMERA
la cámara

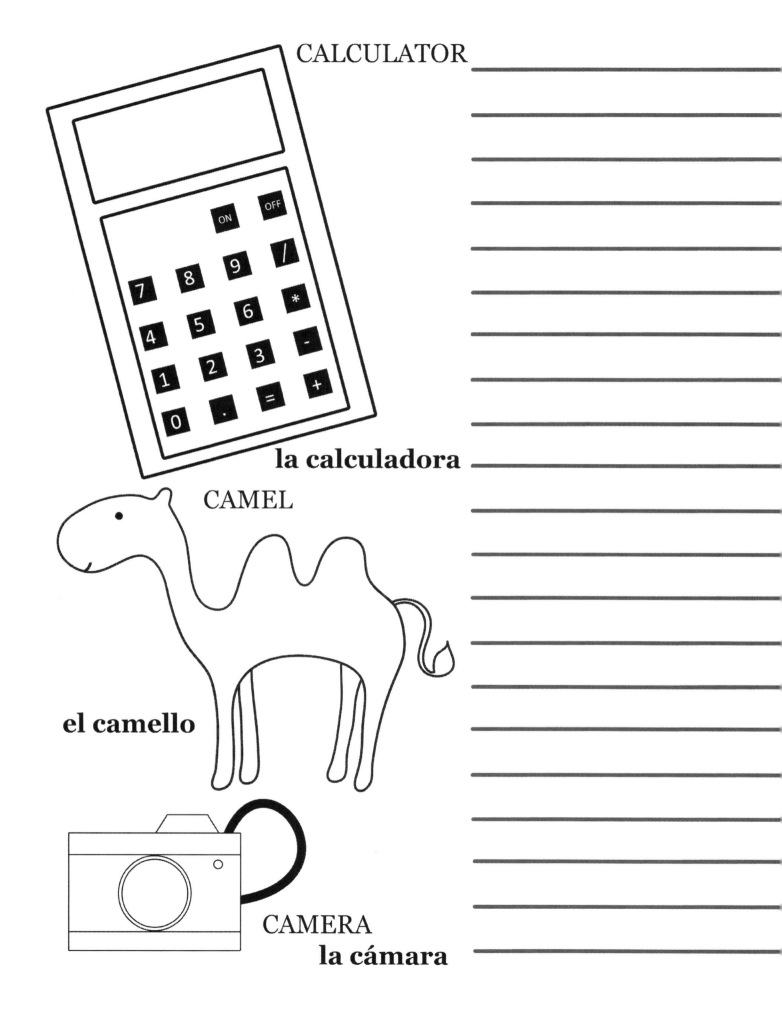

CANDLE

la vela

CANDY

el caramelo

CANDY APPLE

la manzana acaramelada

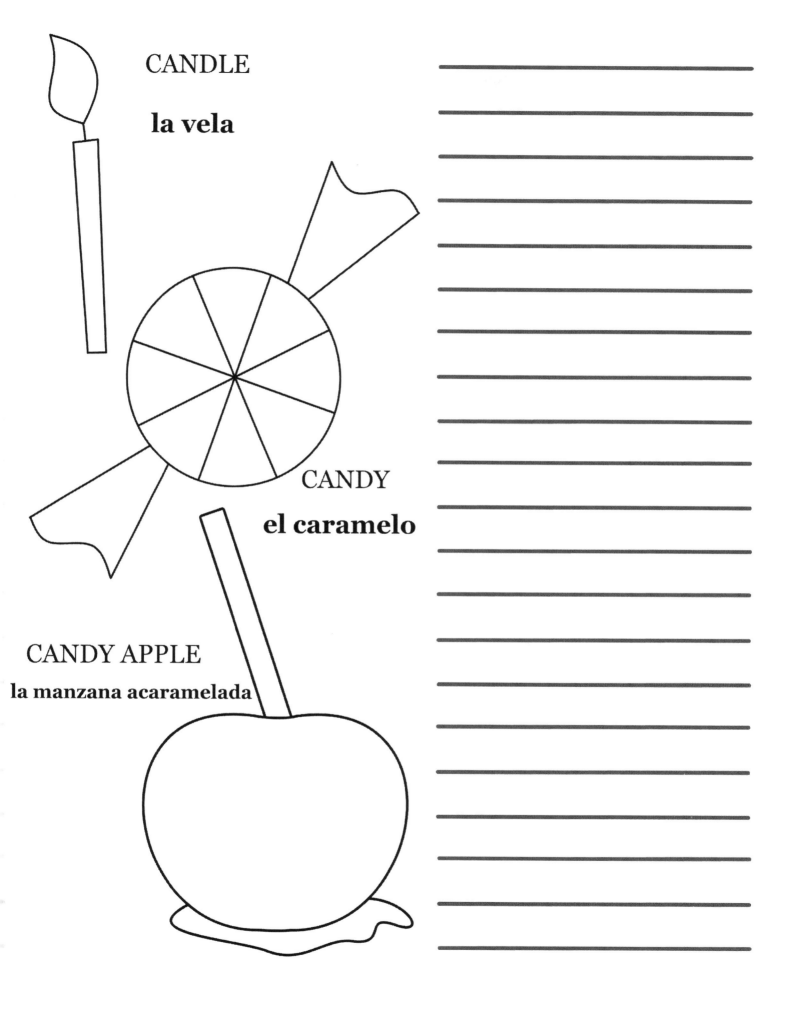

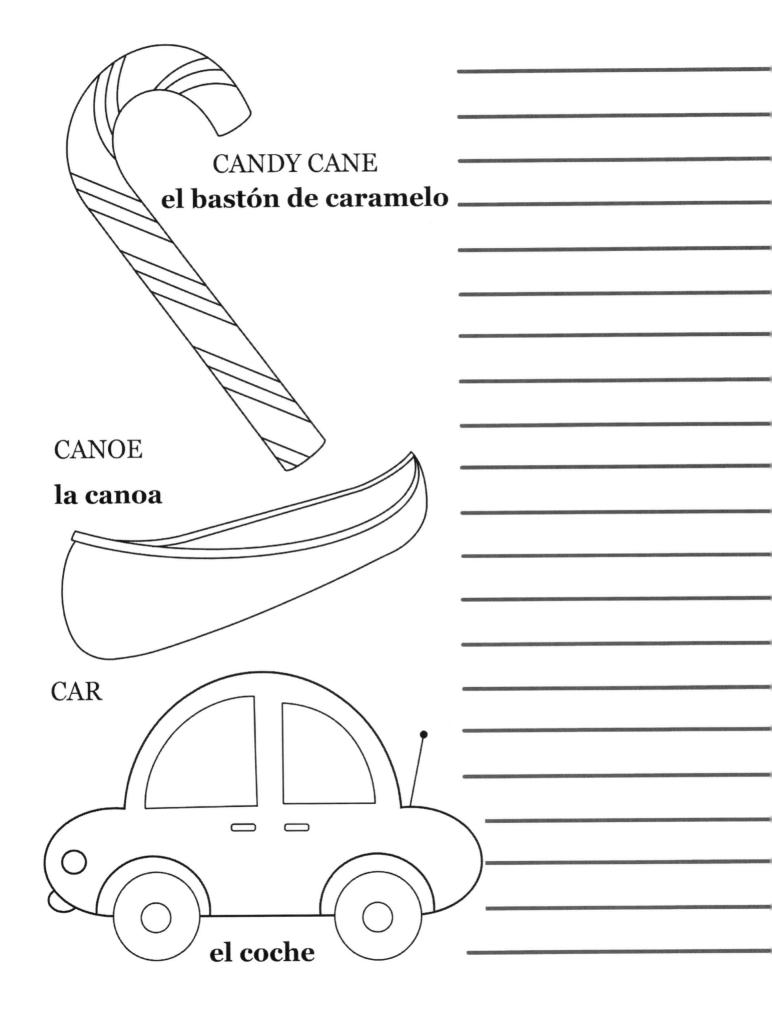

CANDY CANE
el bastón de caramelo

CANOE

la canoa

CAR

el coche

CARRIAGE

el carruaje

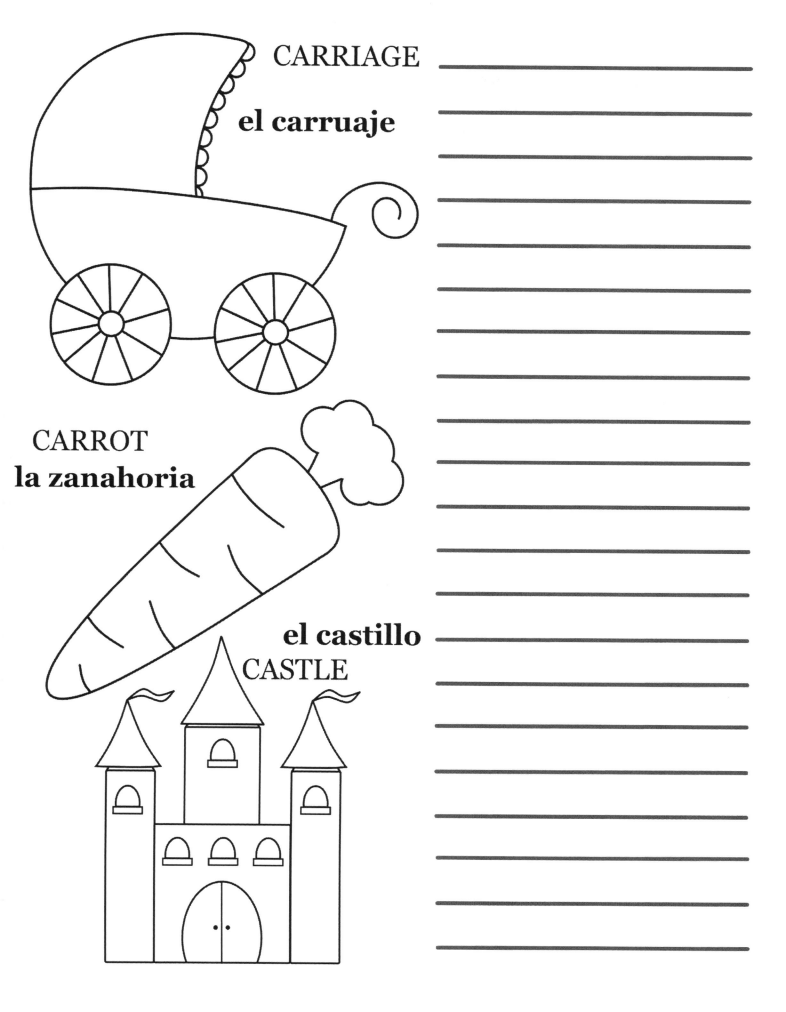

CARROT
la zanahoria

el castillo

CASTLE

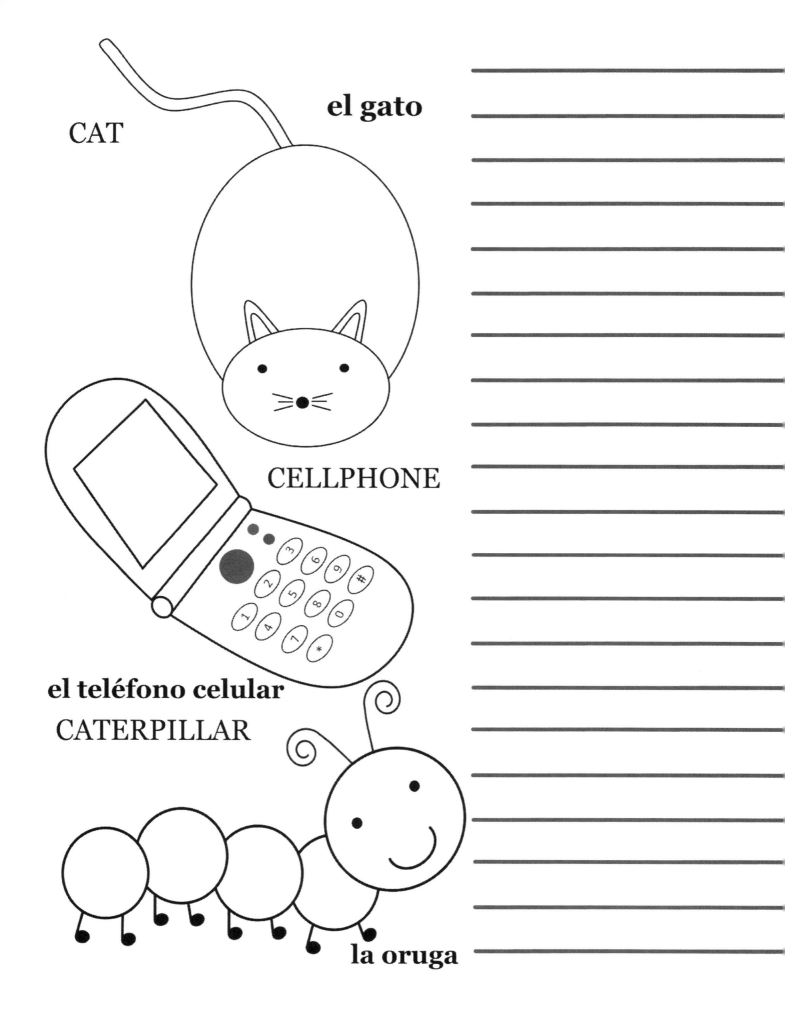

CAT

el gato

CELLPHONE

el teléfono celular

CATERPILLAR

la oruga

CHAMELEON

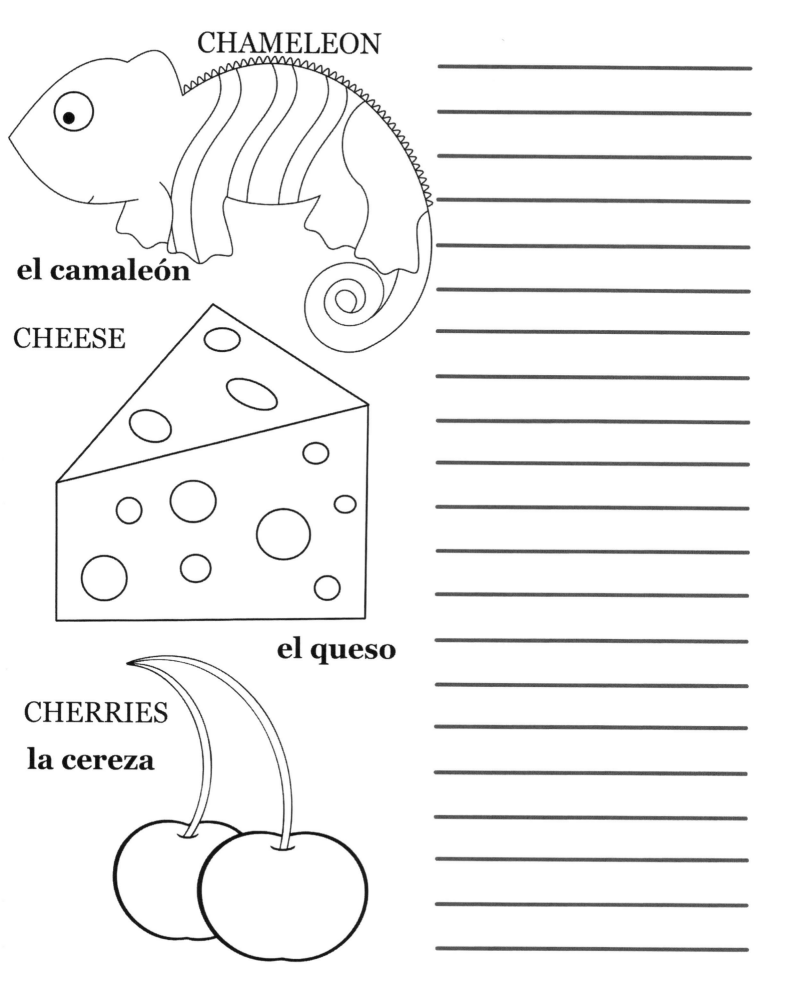

el camaleón

CHEESE

el queso

CHERRIES

la cereza

CHICKEN
el pollo

CHRISTMAS
árbol de Navidad

CHIPMUNK

la ardilla listada

CIRCUS

el circo

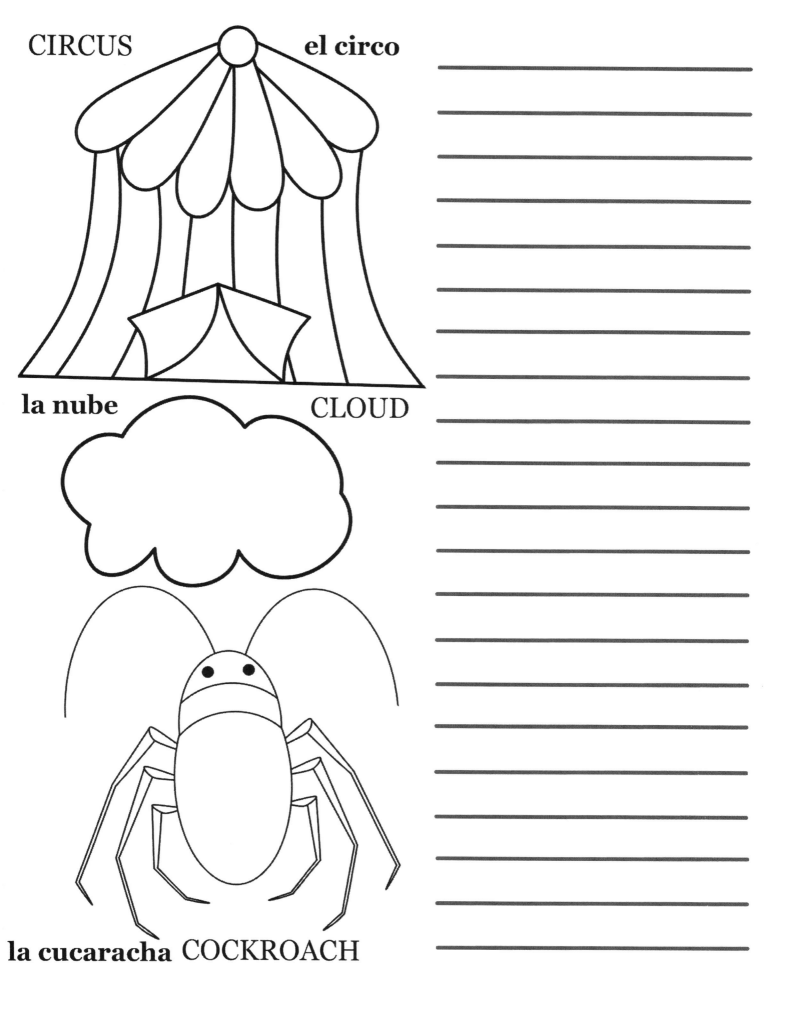

la nube CLOUD

la cucaracha COCKROACH

el coco   COCONUT

COMPASS

la brújula

COMPUTER

la computadora

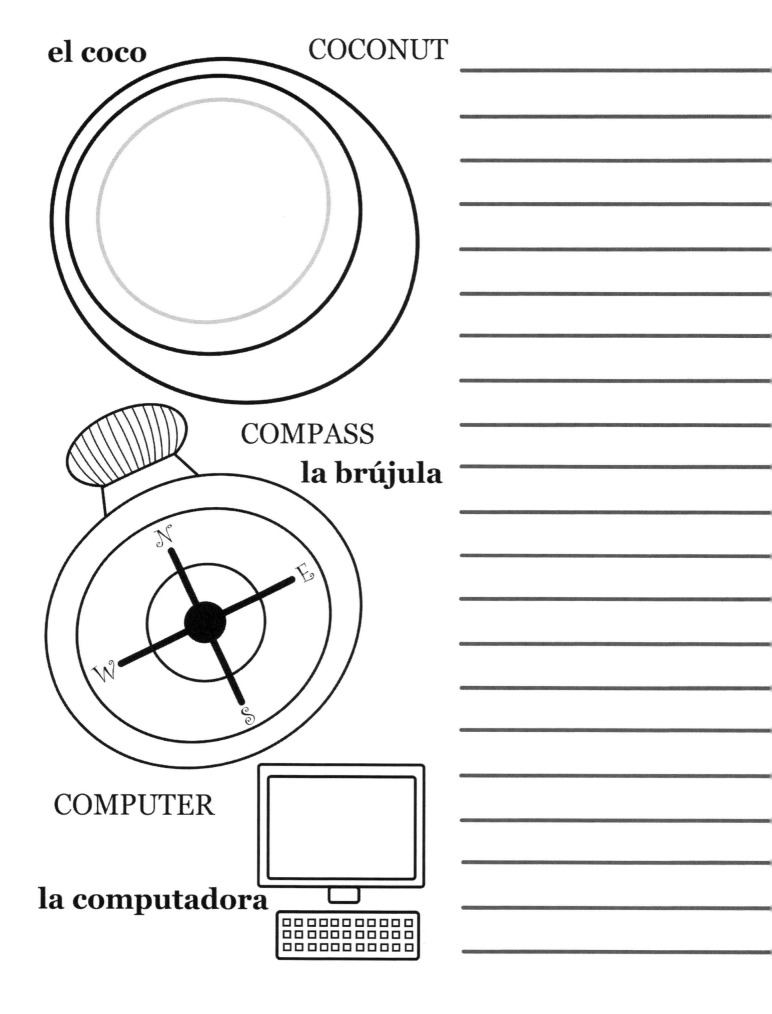

CORN

el maíz

COUGAR

el puma

COW

la vaca

COWBOY BOOT

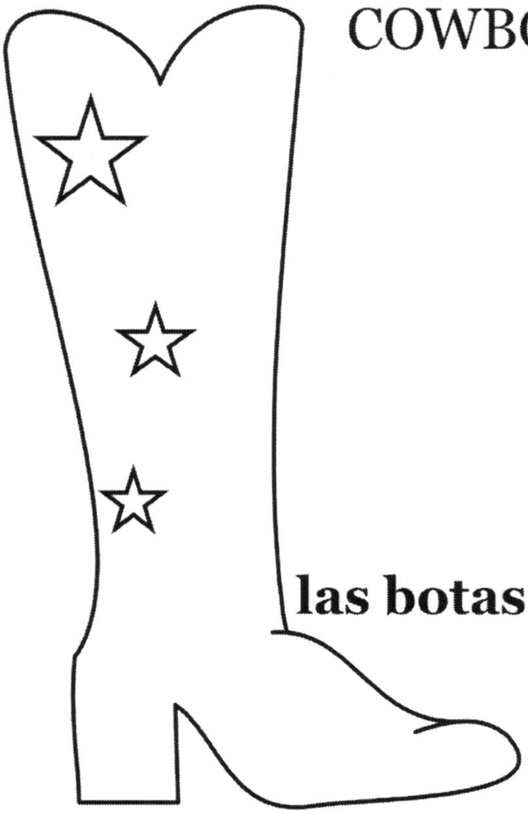

las botas de vaquero

CRAB

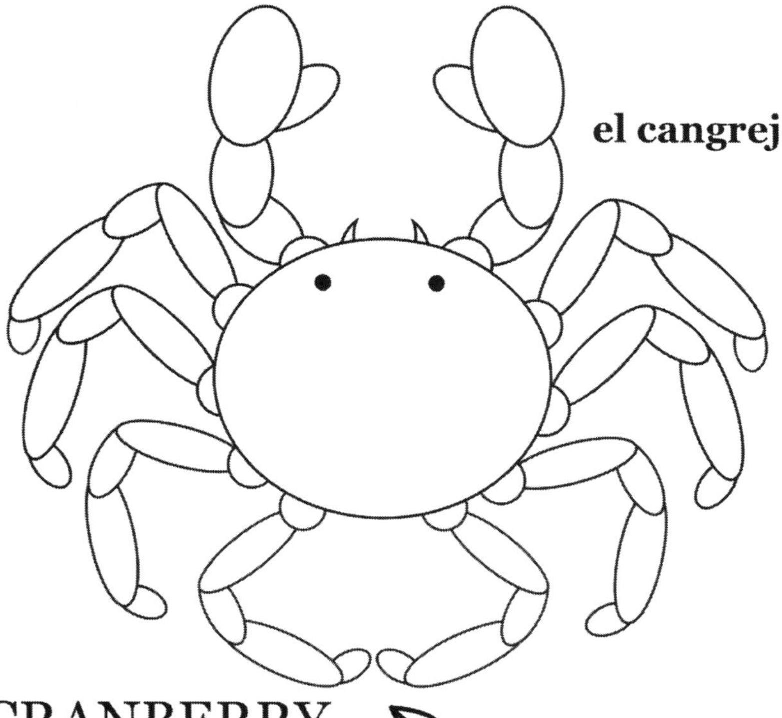

el cangrejo

CRANBERRY

el arándano

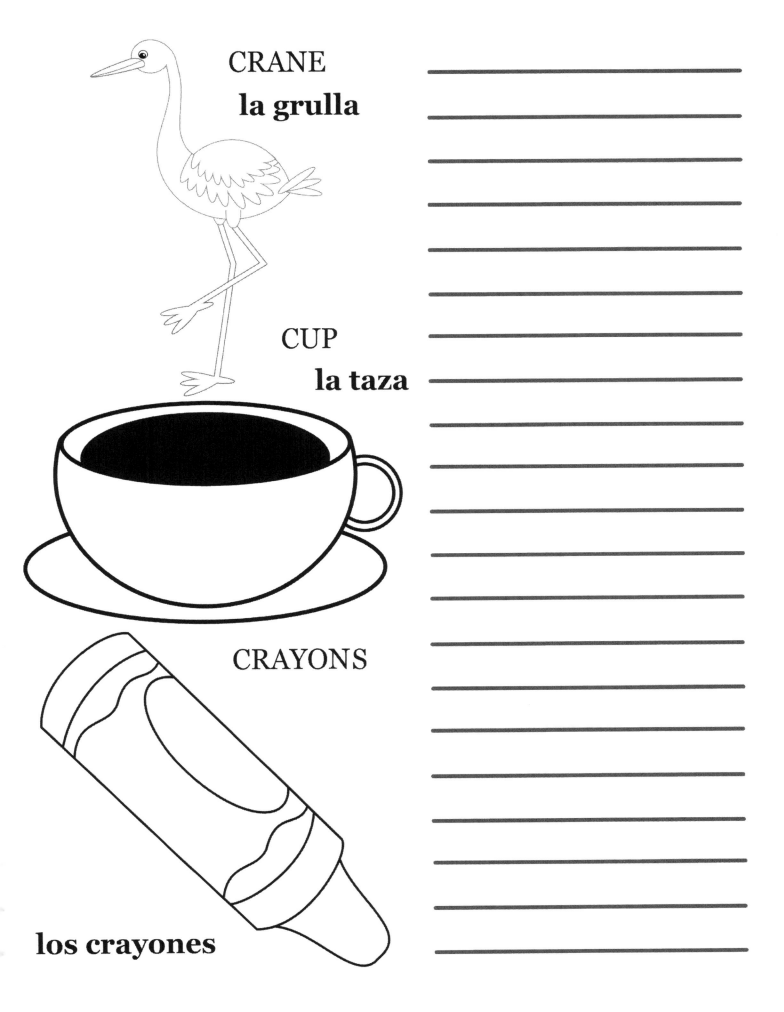

CRANE
la grulla

CUP
la taza

CRAYONS
los crayones

CUPCAKE
la magdalena

DAD
el papá

DINOSAUR
el dinosaurio

DOCTOR

el médico

DOG

el perro

DOLPHIN

el delfín

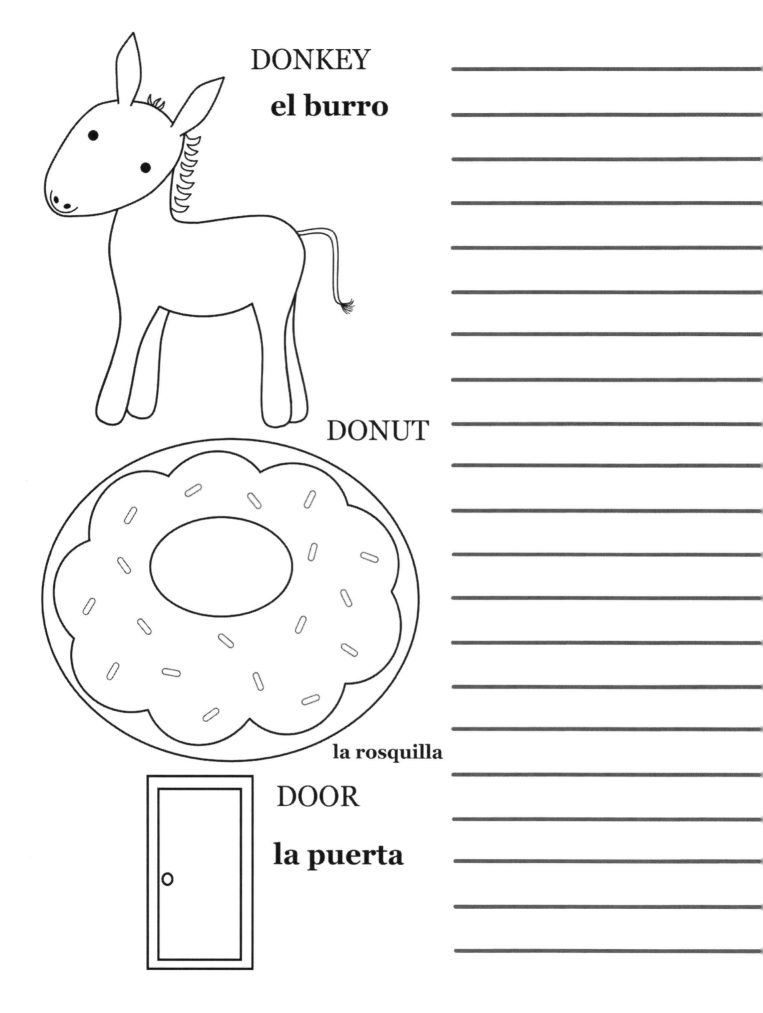

DONKEY
el burro

DONUT

la rosquilla

DOOR

la puerta

DOVE
la paloma

DRAGON
el dragón

la libélula
DRAGONFLY

DRESS
el vestido

DUCK
el pato

DUMPTRUCK **el volquete**

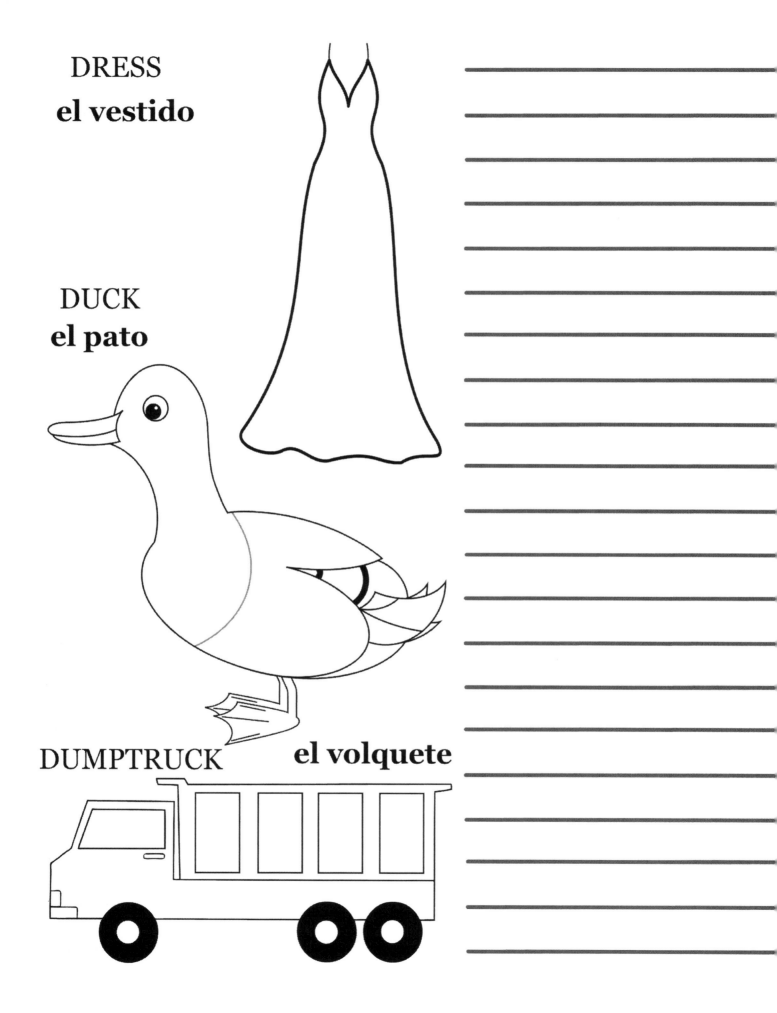

EARRINGS

aretes

EASTER

Pascua

EGG

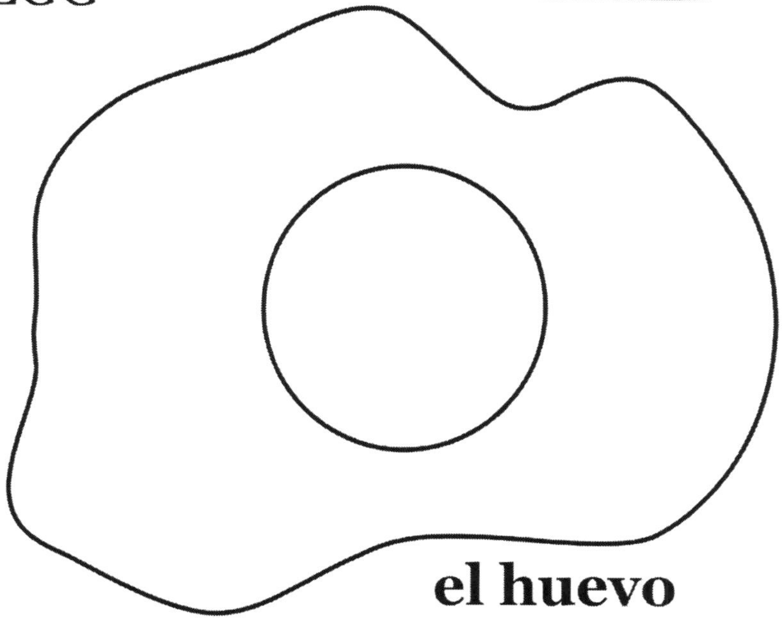

el huevo

EGGPLANT
la berenjena

ELEPHANT
el elefante

ELF
el duende

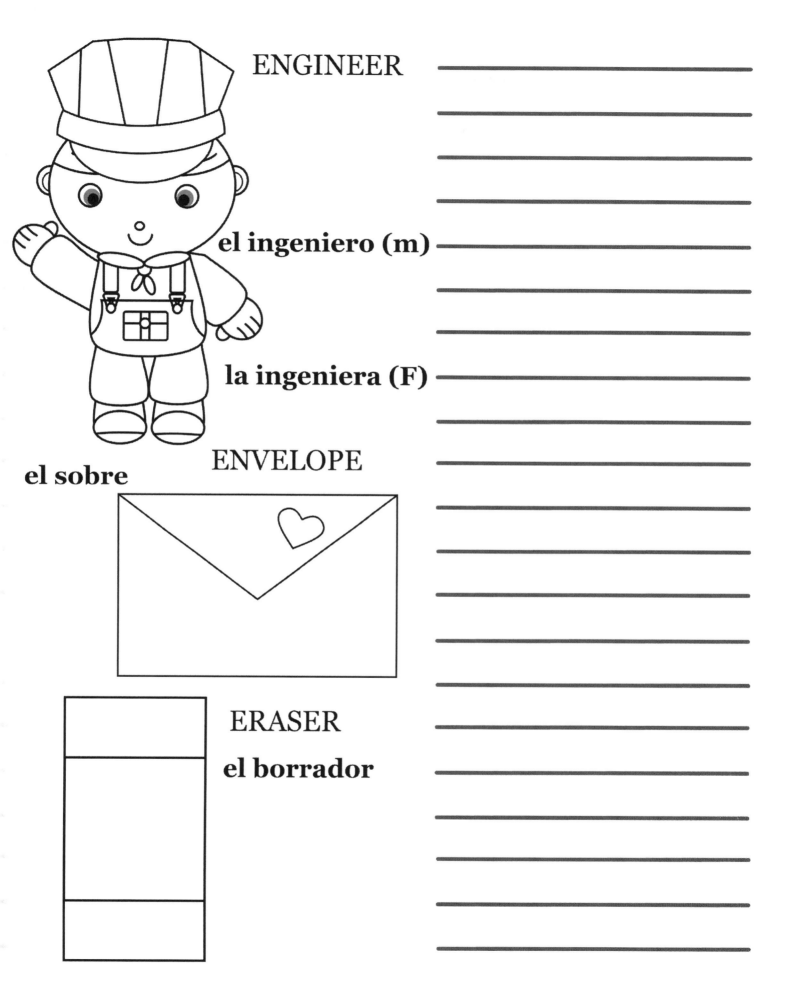

ENGINEER

el ingeniero (m)

la ingeniera (F)

ENVELOPE

el sobre

ERASER

el borrador

EVENING

la tarde

FAIRY

el hada

FAMILY

la familia

FAN   el ventilador

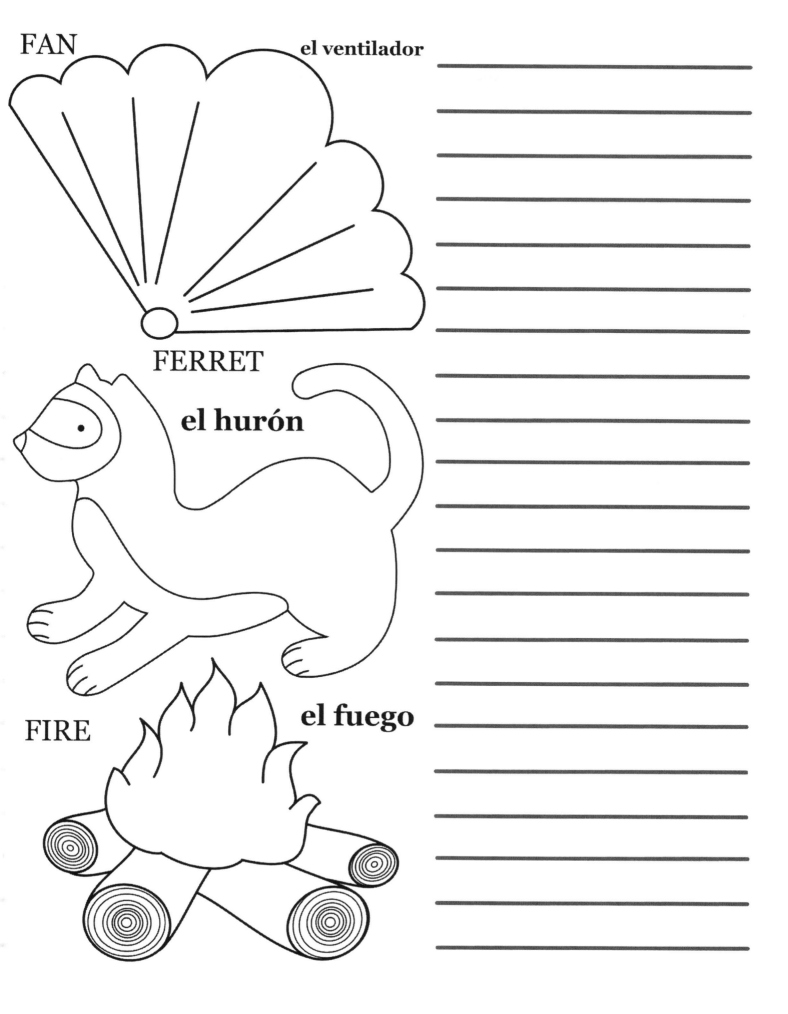

FERRET

el hurón

FIRE   el fuego

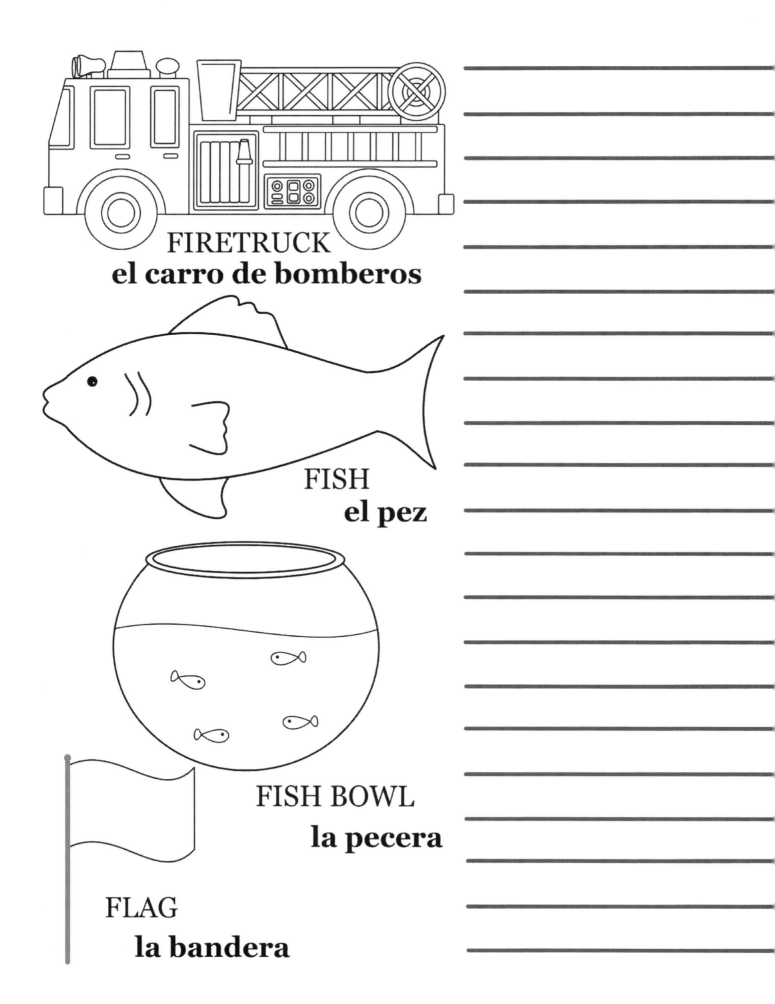

FIRETRUCK
el carro de bomberos

FISH
el pez

FISH BOWL
la pecera

FLAG
la bandera

FLAMINGO

el flamenco

FLOWER **la flor**

FLY **la mosca**

FOOTBALL

el fútbol

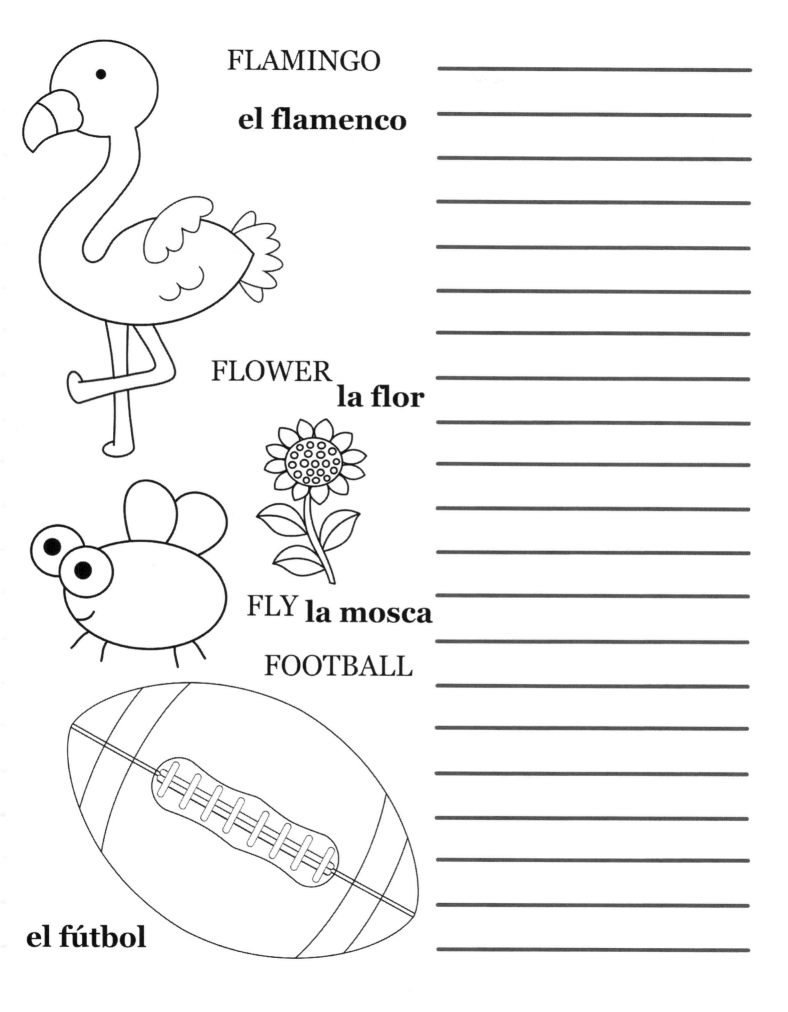

FORK el tenedor

FOX

el zorro

FRIDGE
la nevera

FRIEND

el amigo
(m)
la amiga
(f)

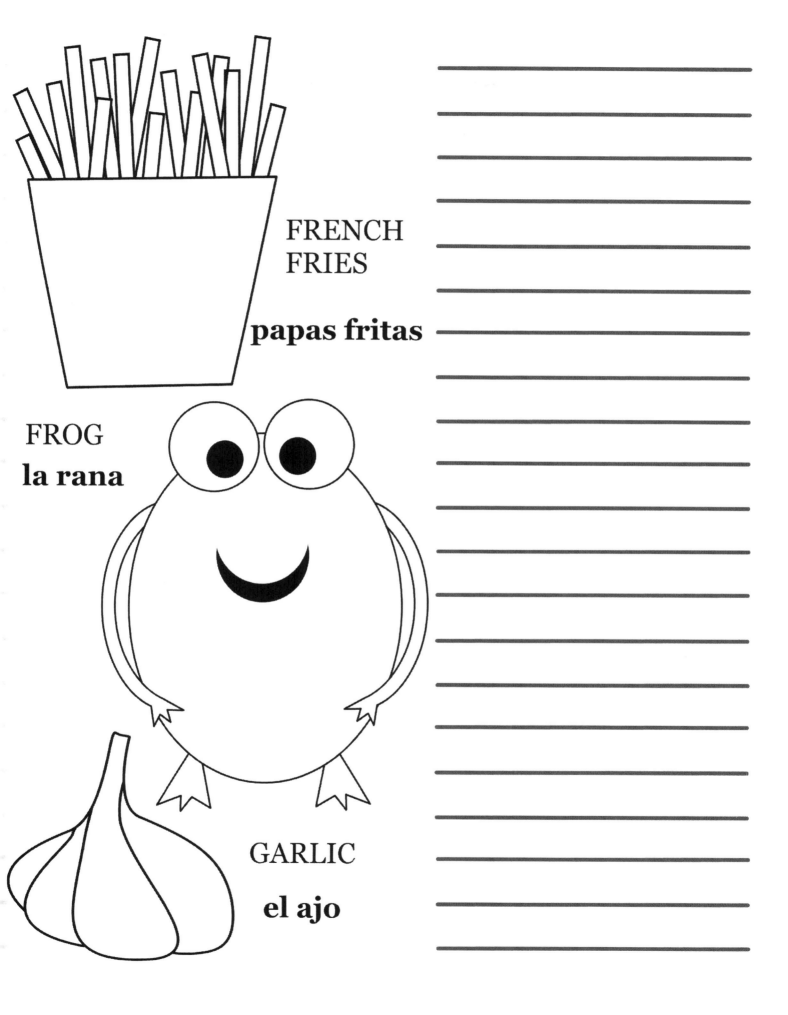

FRENCH
FRIES

papas fritas

FROG
la rana

GARLIC

el ajo

GEESE
los gansos

GHOST

el fantasma

GIRAFFE
la jirafa

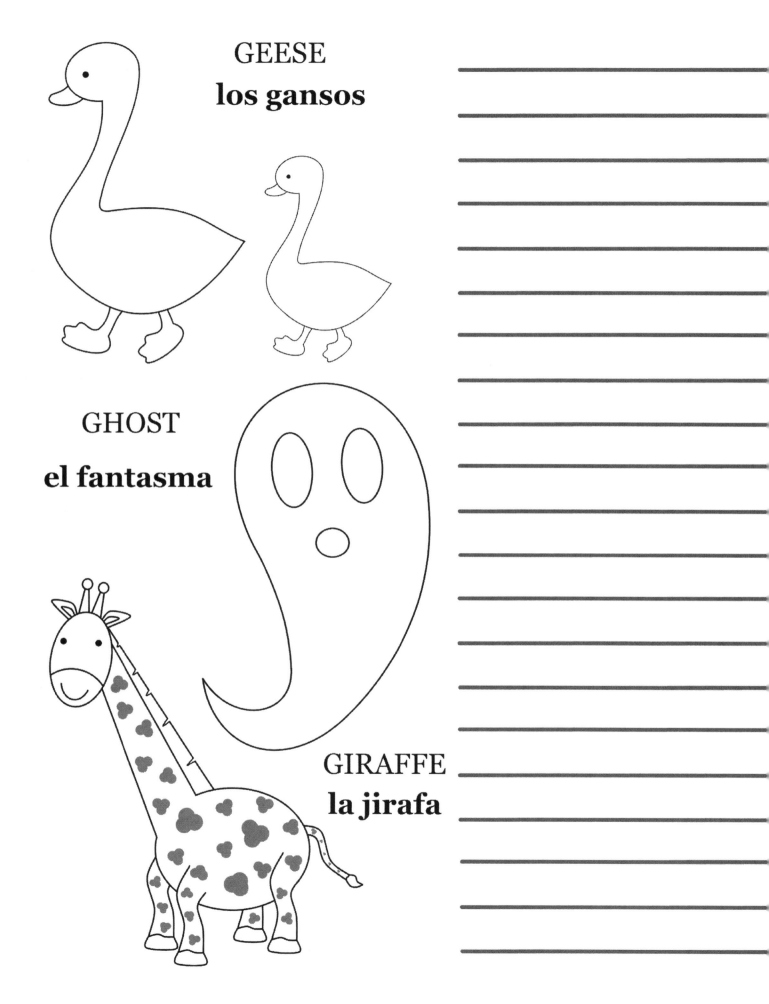

GLASS
el vaso

GLOVE
el guante

GLASSES
las gafas

GOAT
la cabra

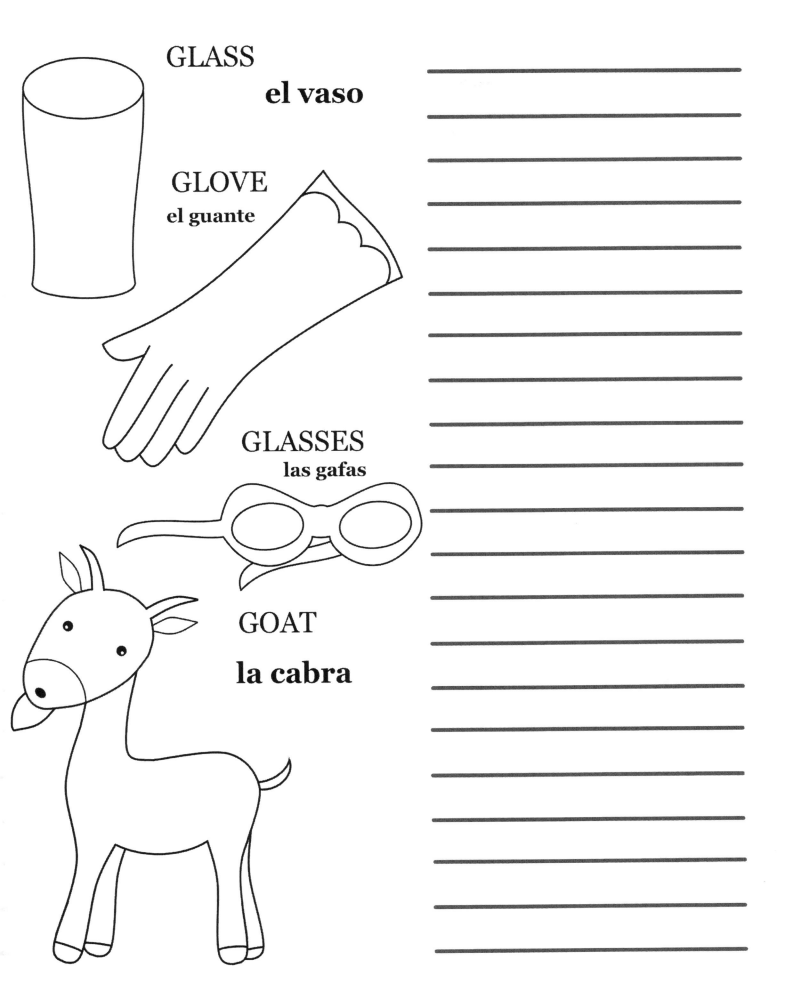

GOBLIN

el duende

GOLF

el golf

GORILLA

el/la gorila

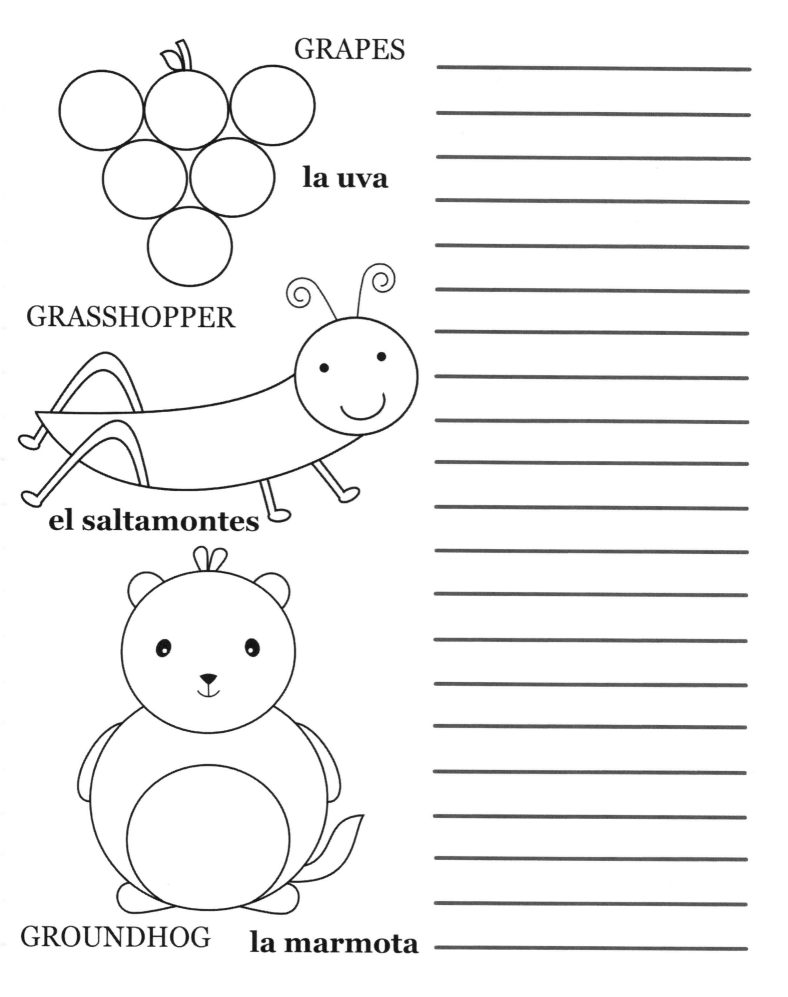

GRAPES

la uva

GRASSHOPPER

el saltamontes

GROUNDHOG   **la marmota**

GUINEA PIG   el conejillo de indias

HAIR BRUSH

cepillo de pelo

HAIR DRYER

el secador de pelo

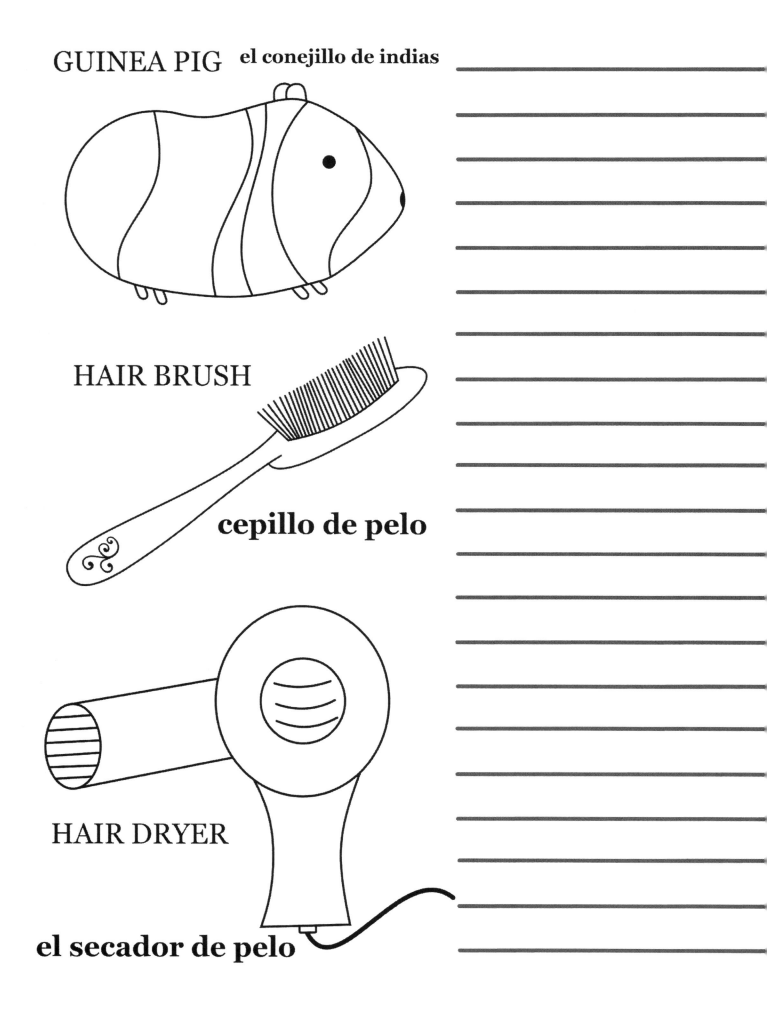

HALLOWEEN

**víspera del día
de Todos los
Santos**

HAMBURGER

la hamburguesa

HAMSTER

el hámster

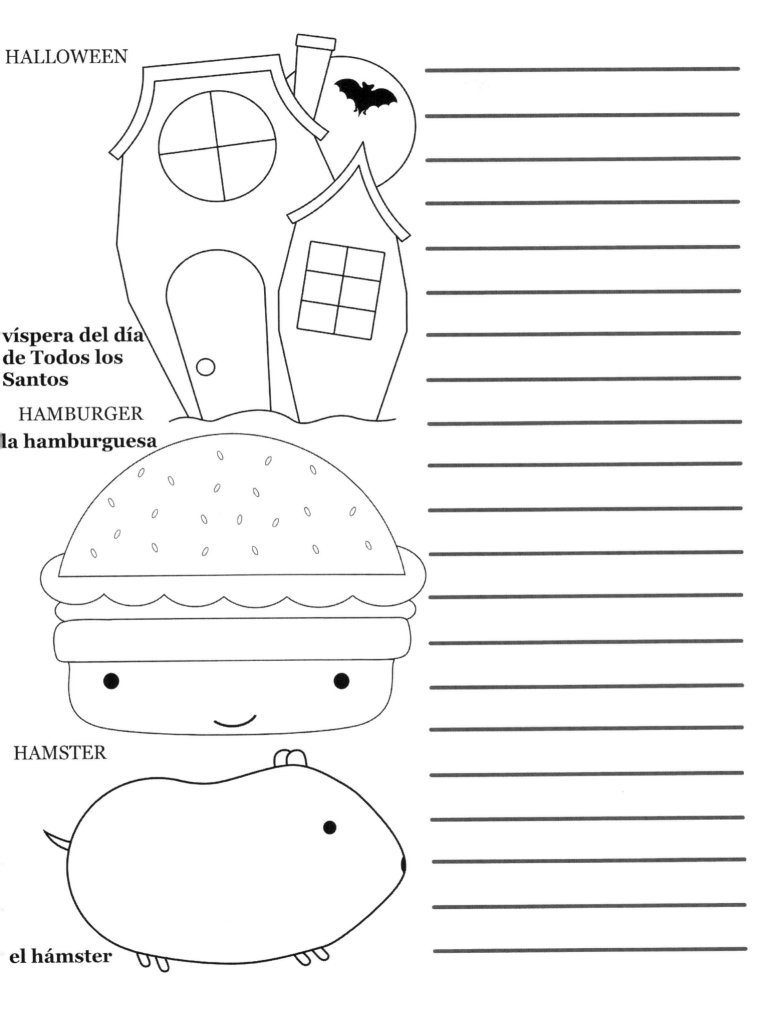

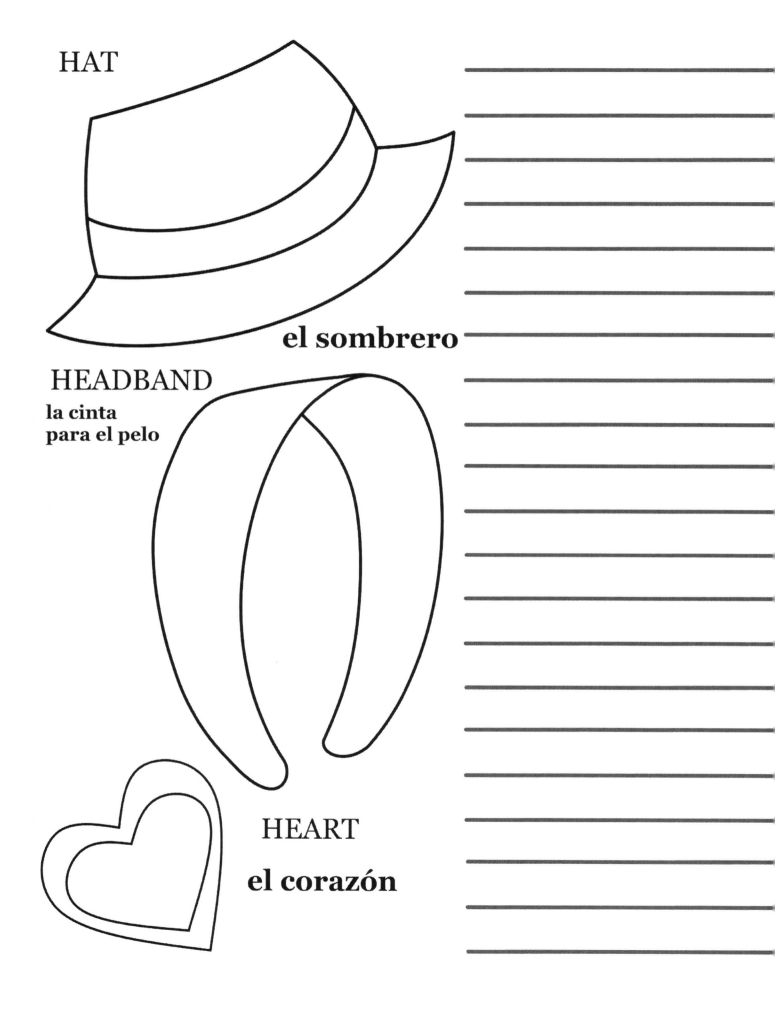

HAT

el sombrero

HEADBAND

la cinta
para el pelo

HEART

el corazón

HEDGEHOG   el erizo

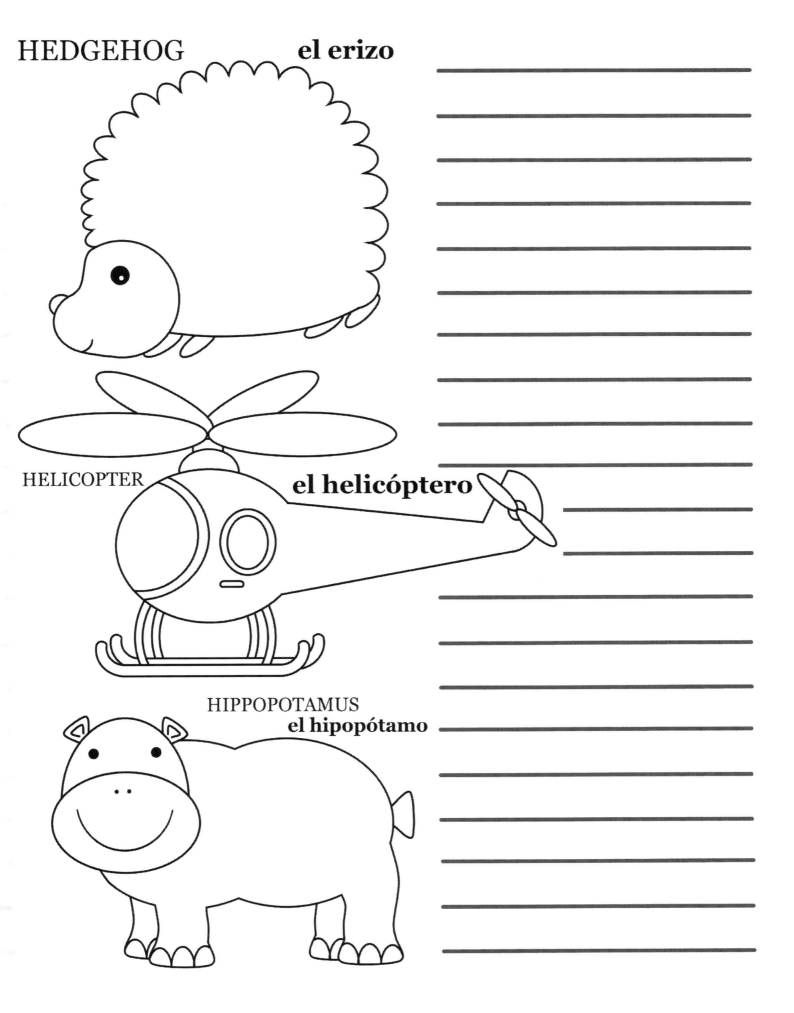

HELICOPTER   el helicóptero

HIPPOPOTAMUS
el hipopótamo

HOCKEY
el hockey

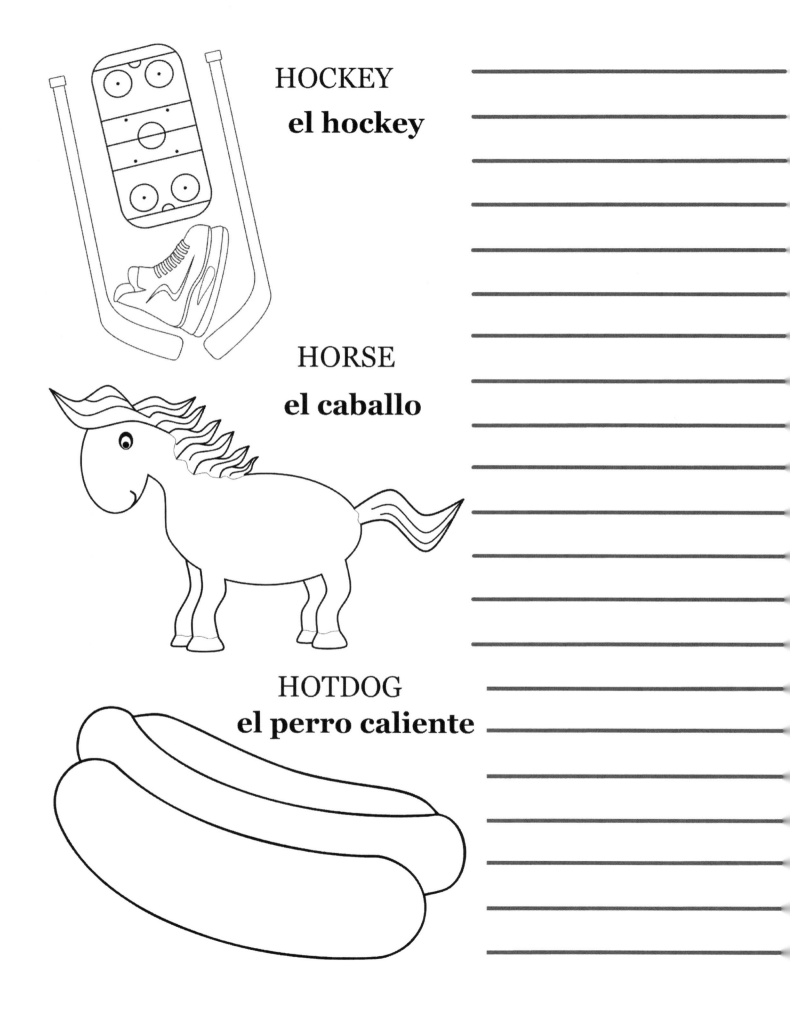

HORSE
el caballo

HOTDOG
el perro caliente

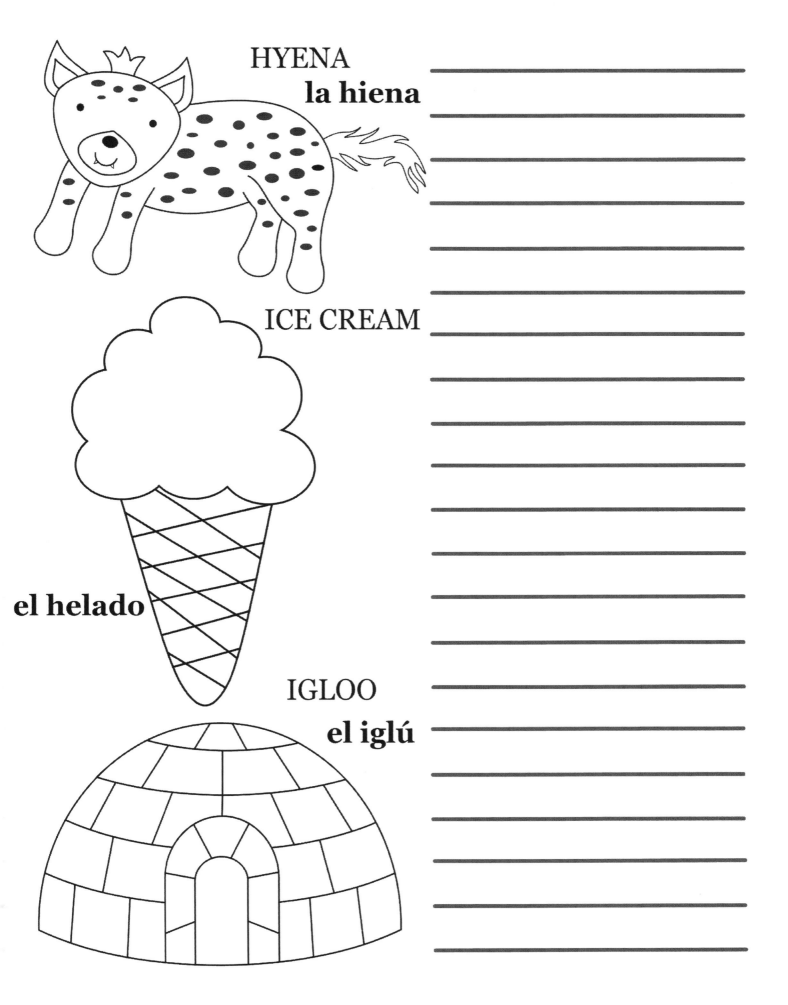

HYENA
la hiena

ICE CREAM

el helado

IGLOO
el iglú

IGUANA

la iguana

JAGUAR

el jaguar

JALAPENO

jalapeño pepper

JELLYBEAN
la gominola

practicar motociclismo acuático
JETSKI

KANGAROO

el canguro

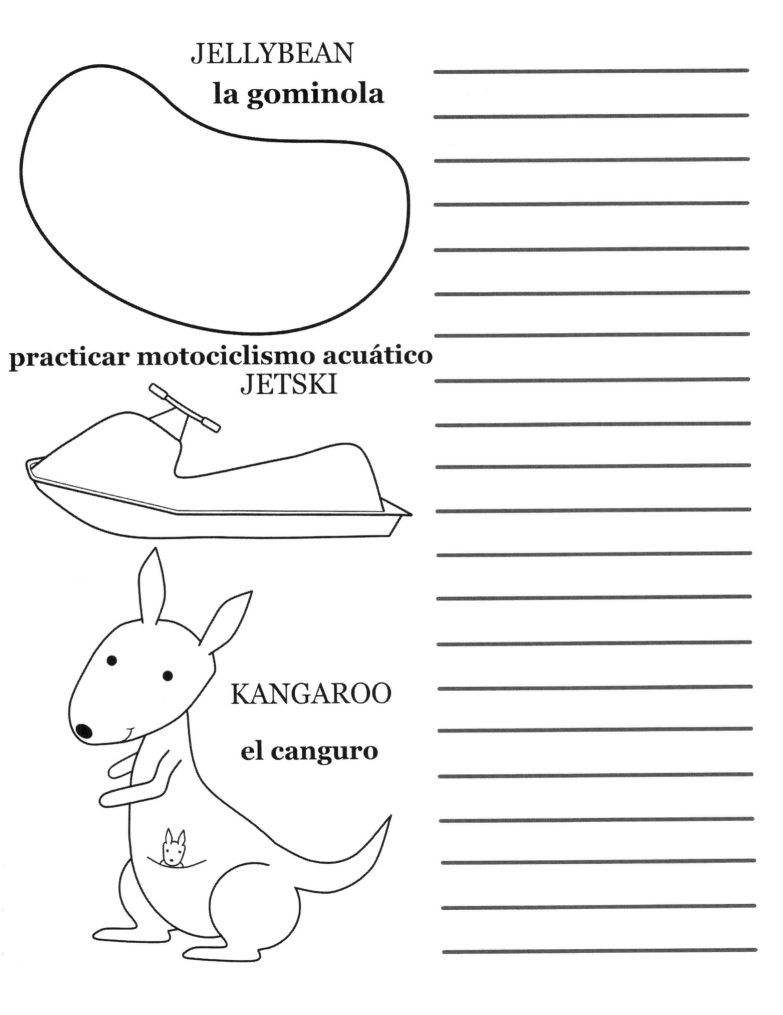

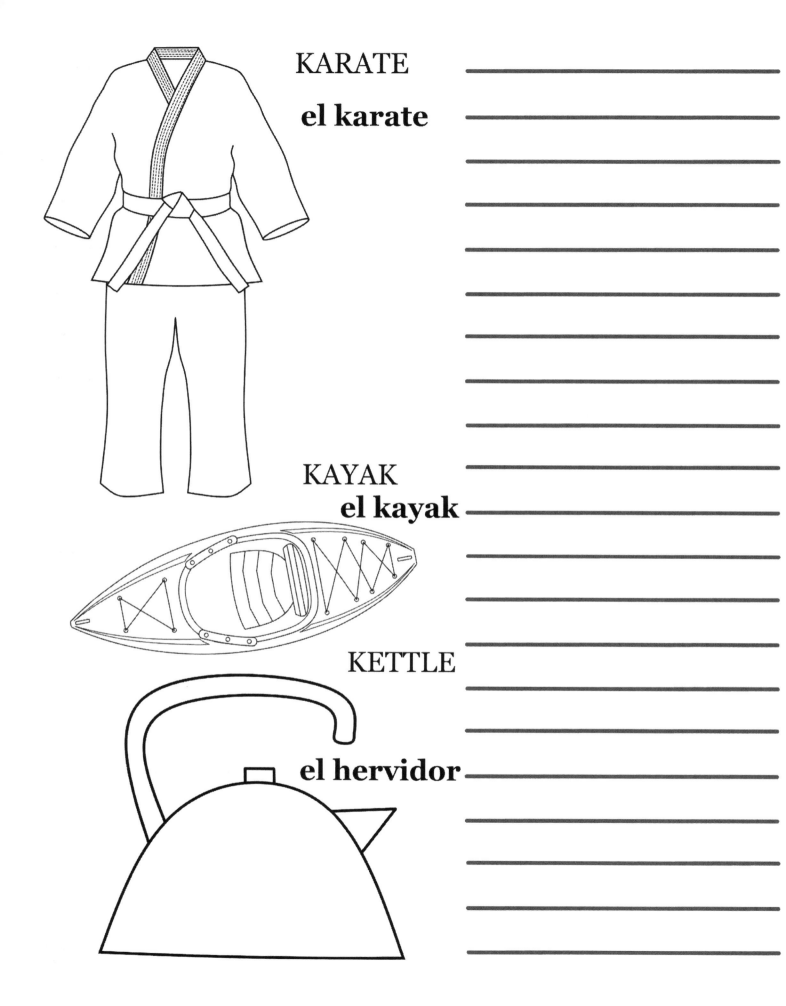

KARATE

el karate

KAYAK

el kayak

KETTLE

el hervidor

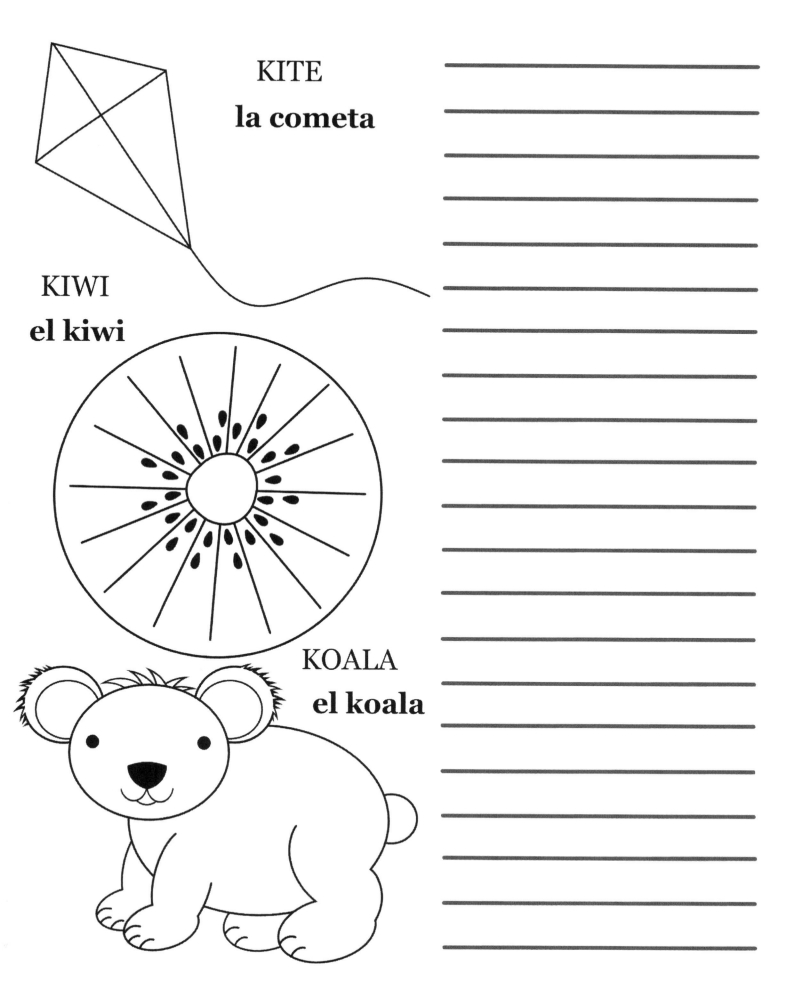

KITE
la cometa

KIWI
el kiwi

KOALA
el koala

LADDER

la escalera

LADYBUG

la mariquita

LEAF

la hoja

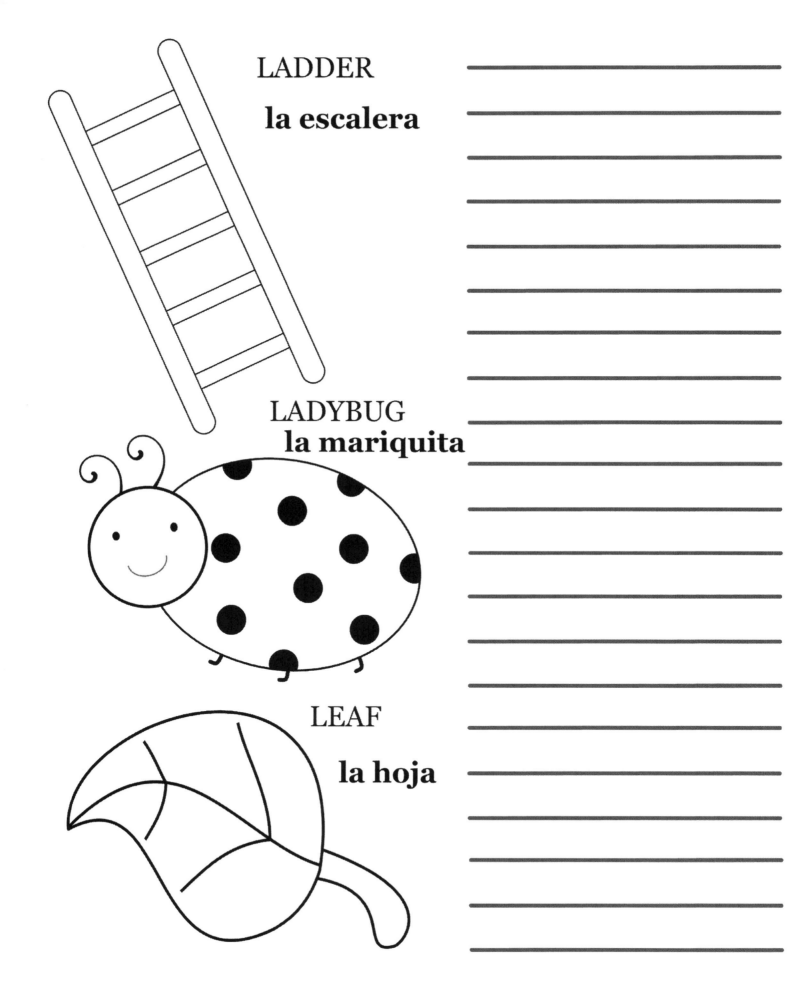

LEMON

el limón

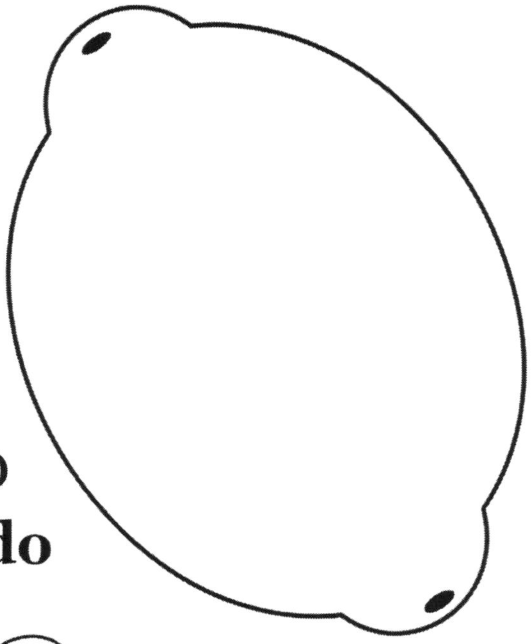

LEOPARD

el leopardo

LIFEJACKET

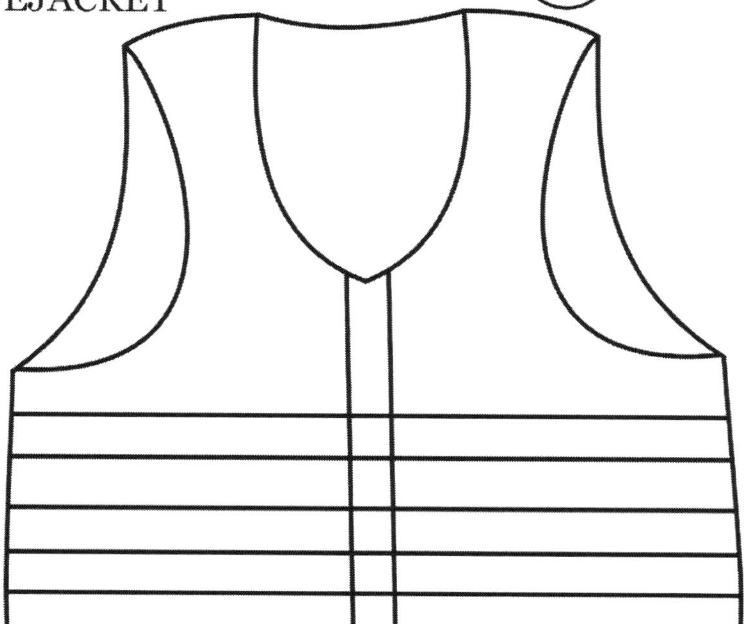

el chaleco salvavidas

LIGHTHOUSE **el faro**

LION **el león**

LIPS **el labio**

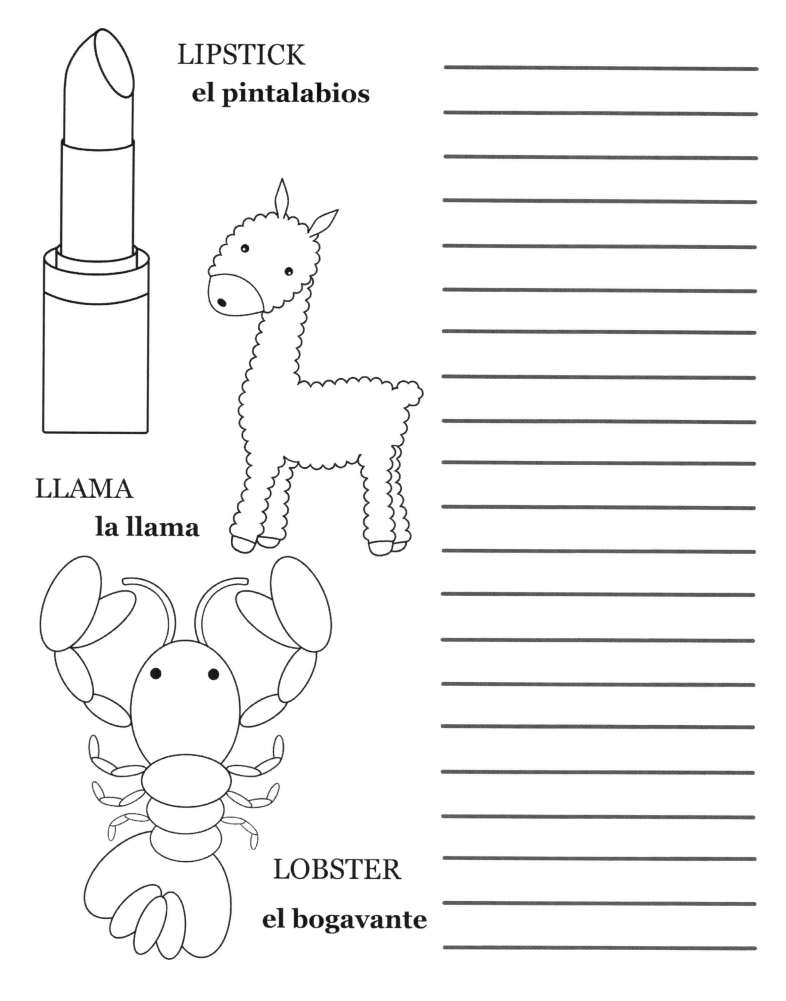

LIPSTICK
el pintalabios

LLAMA
la llama

LOBSTER
el bogavante

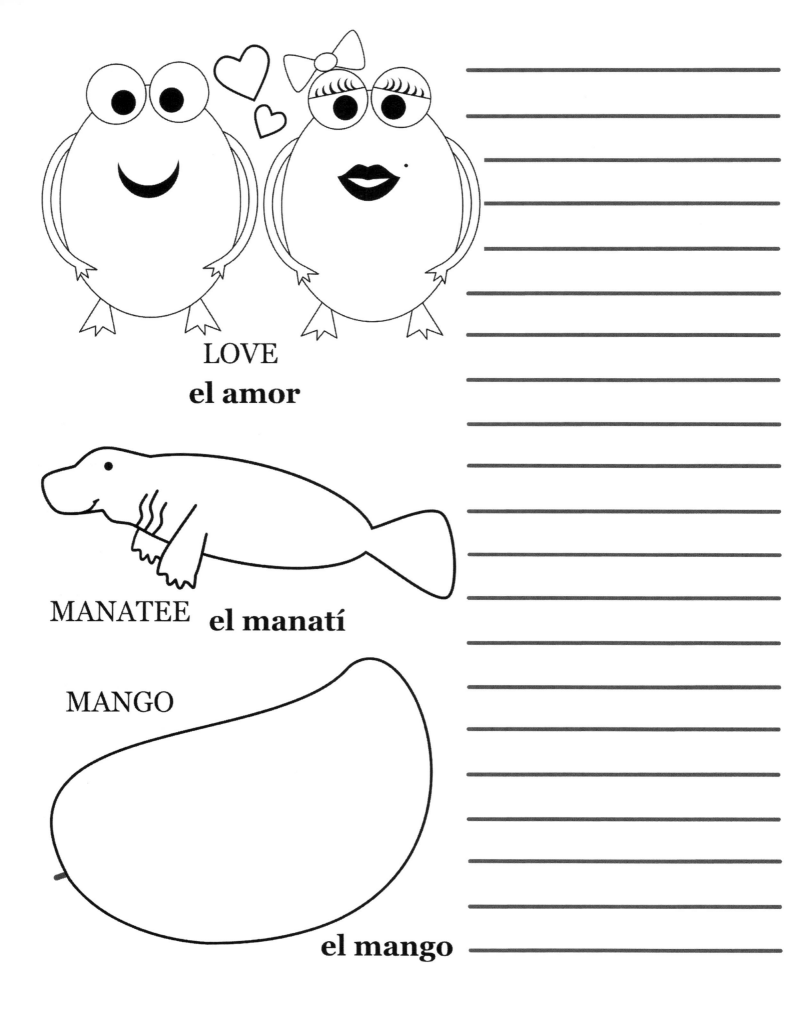

LOVE

el amor

MANATEE **el manatí**

MANGO

el mango

MARSHMALLOW
el malvavisco

MEERKAT
la suricata

MERMAID
la sirena

MIRROR
el espejo

MOM

la mamá

MONKEY

el mono

MONSTER

el monstruo

MOON

la luna

MOOSE

el alce

MORNING

la mañana

MOTORCYCLE
la motocicleta

MOUSE
el ratón

MUSHROOM
el hongo

NARWHAL **el narval**

NECKLACE
el collar

NET
la red

OCTOPUS
el pulpo

OSTRICH
el avestruz

OTTER
la nutria

OVEN MITT
el guante para horno

OWL
el búho

PAINT BRUSH
el pincel

la palmera   PALM TREE

PANDA

El panda

PAN
la sartén

PANTHER
la pantera

PANTS
los pantalones

PARROT
el loro

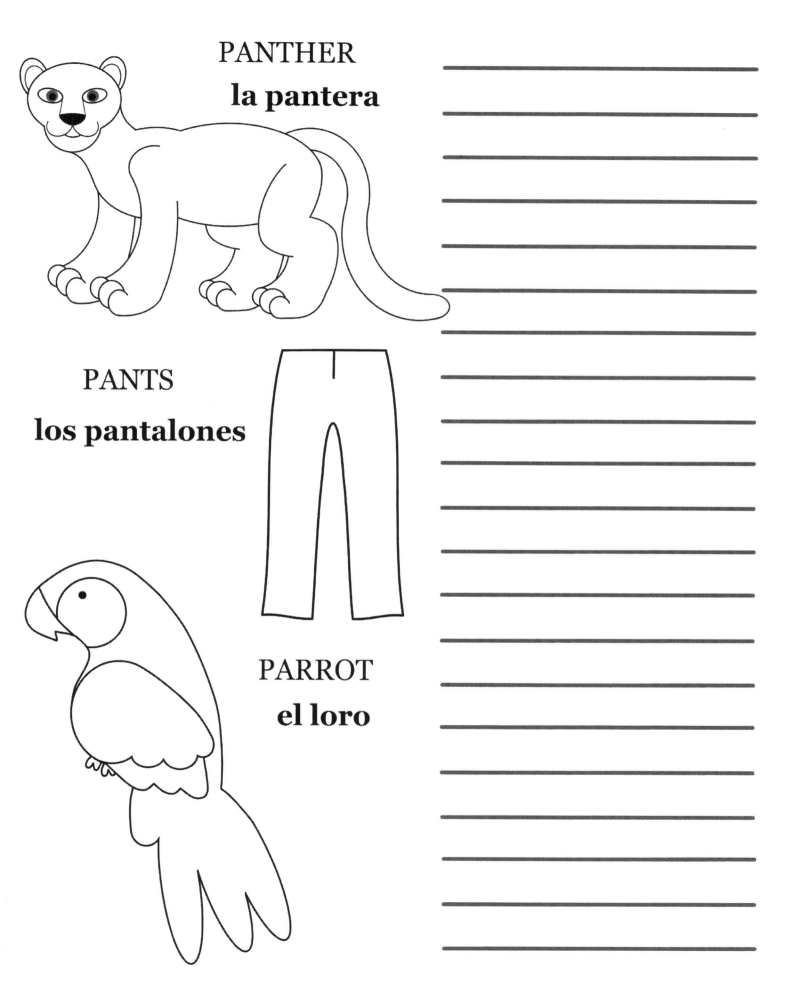

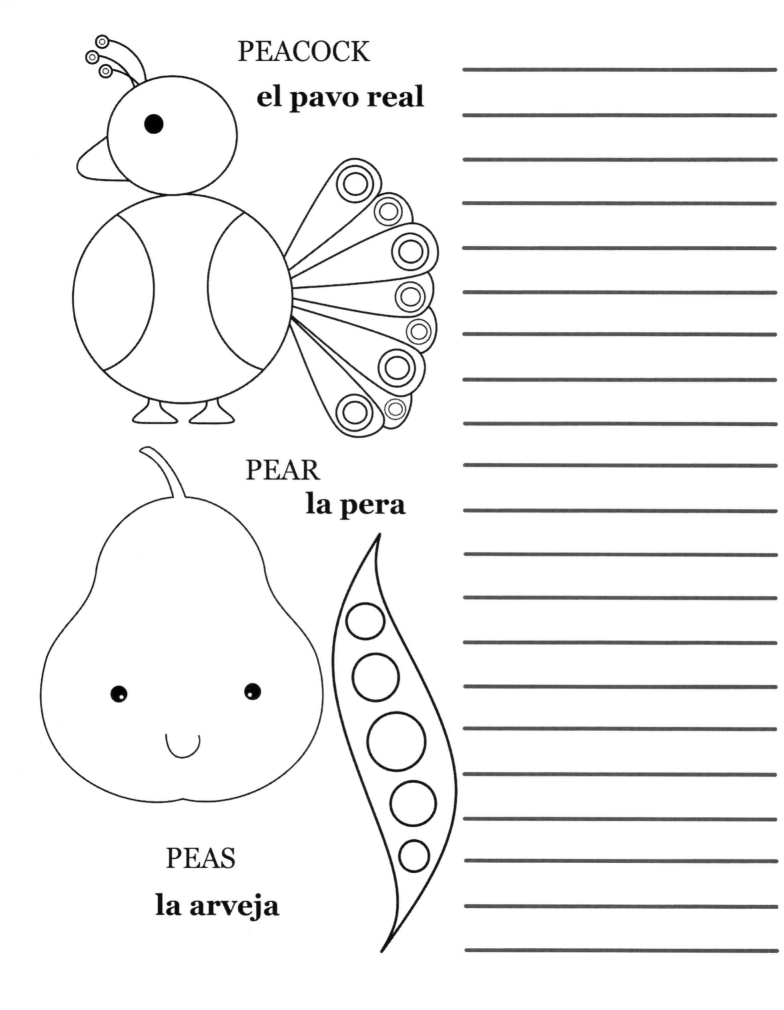

PEACOCK
el pavo real

PEAR
la pera

PEAS
la arveja

PELICAN
el pelícano

PENCIL **el lápiz**

PENGUIN **el pingüino**

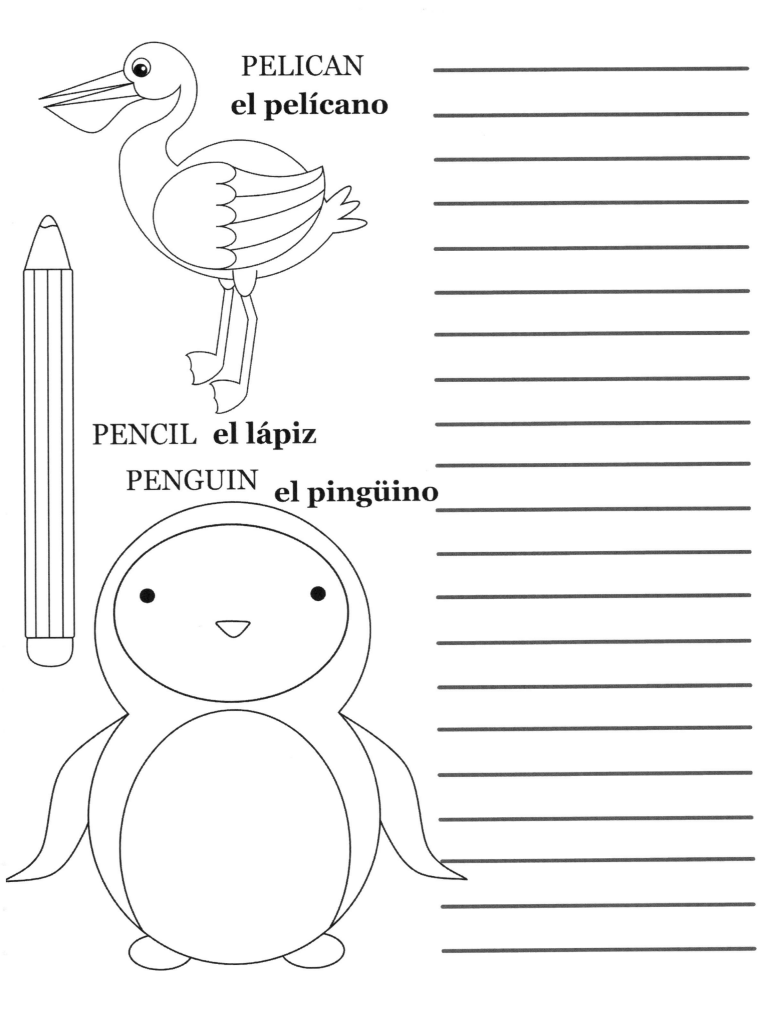

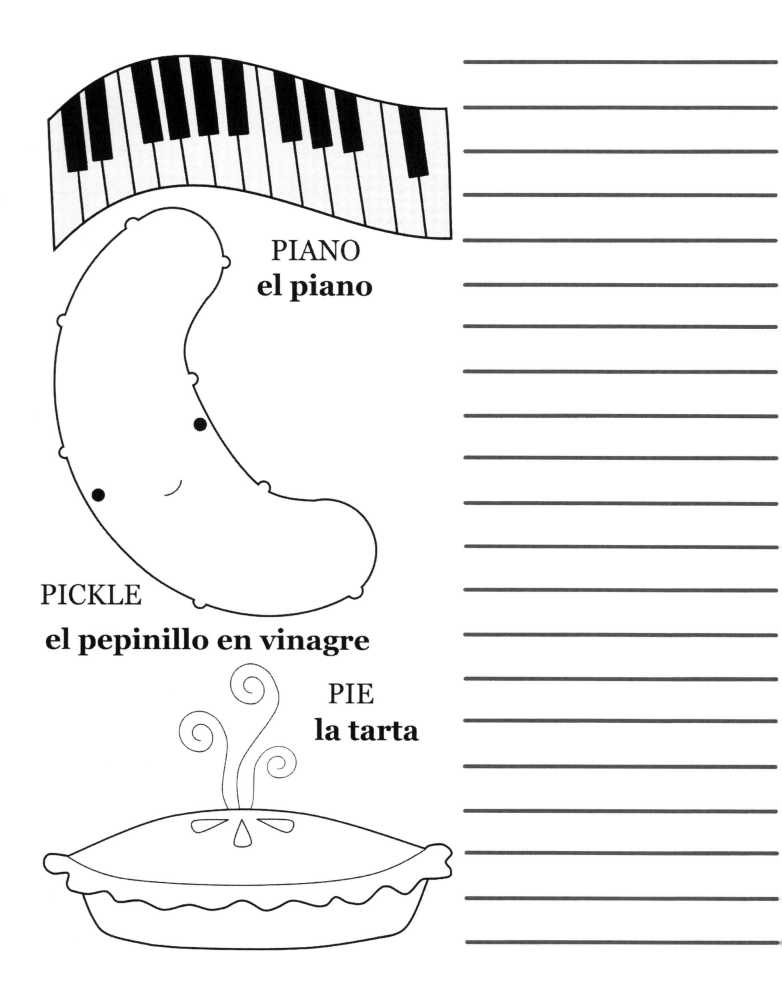

PIANO
el piano

PICKLE
el pepinillo en vinagre

PIE
la tarta

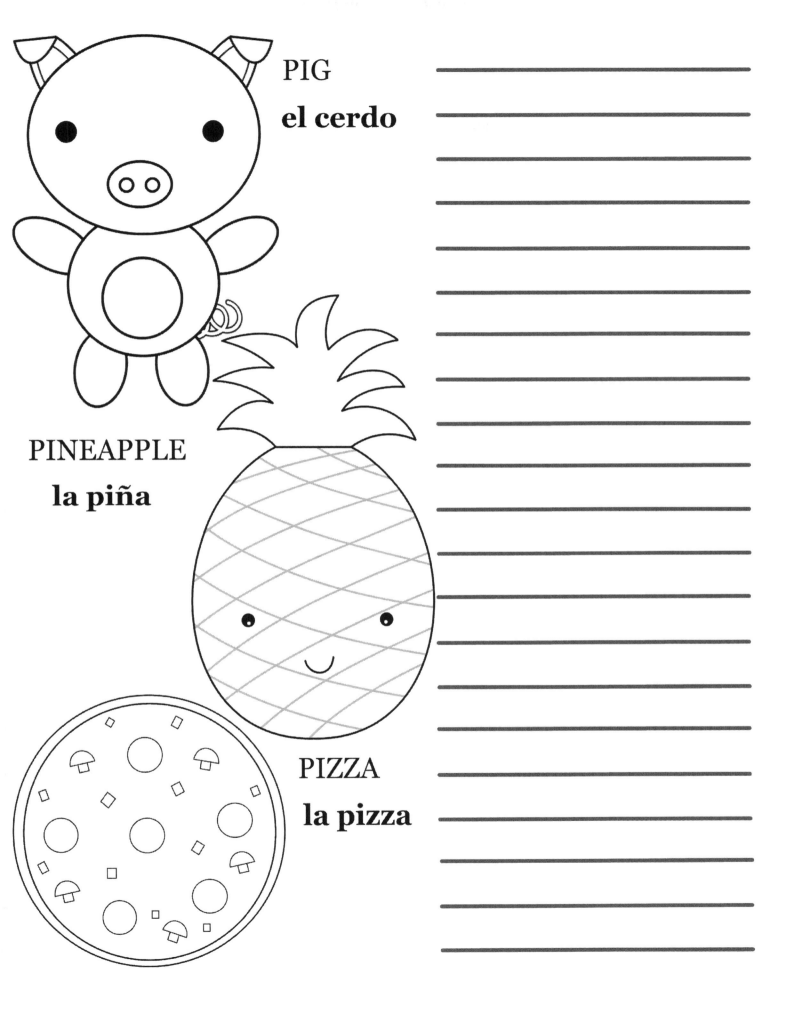

PIG
el cerdo

PINEAPPLE
la piña

PIZZA
la pizza

PLANET

el planeta

PLATE

el plato

PLATYPUS

el ornitorrinco

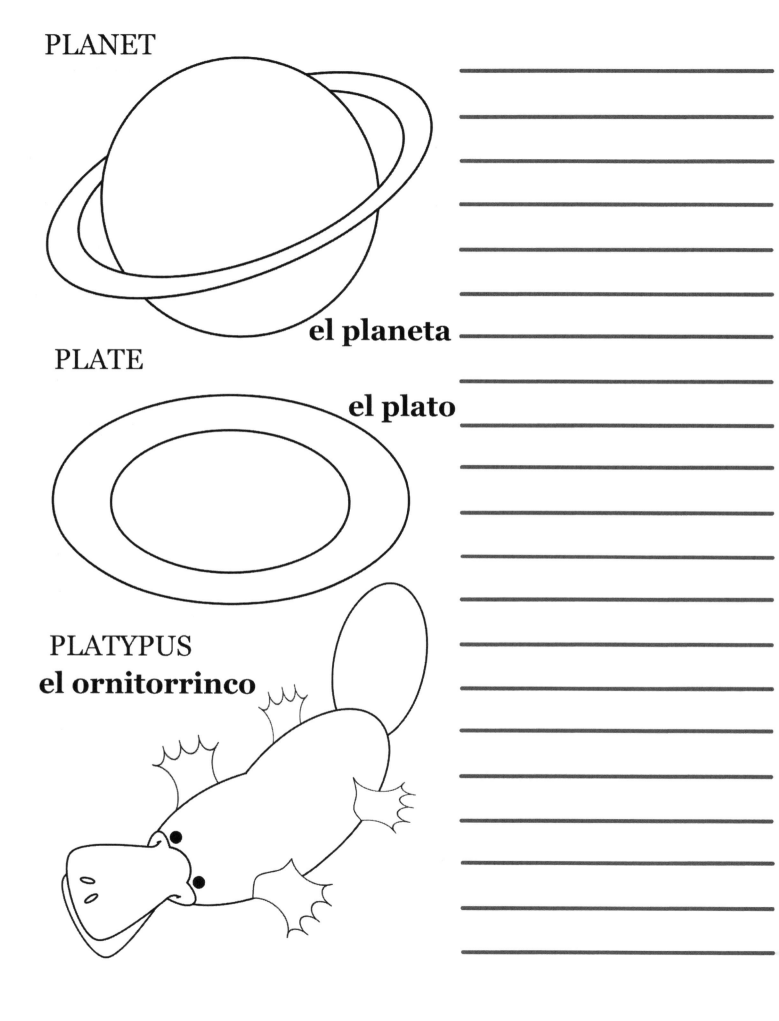

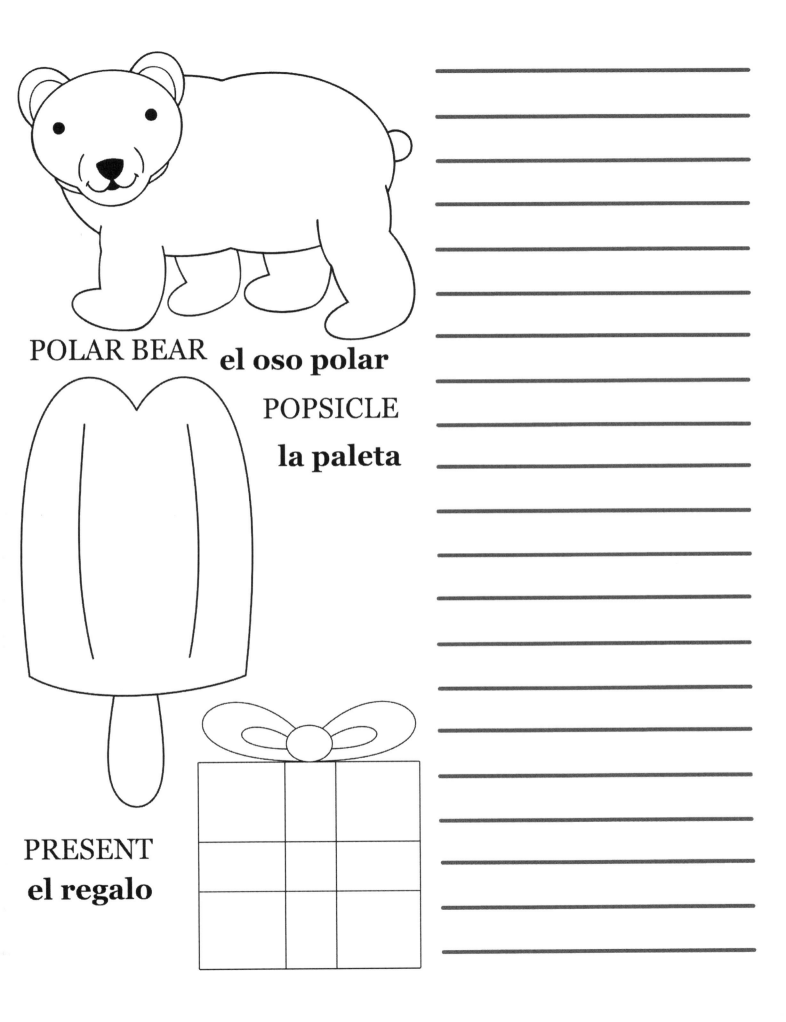

POLAR BEAR **el oso polar**

POPSICLE

la paleta

PRESENT

el regalo

PRINCESS **la princesa**

PUMPKIN

la calabaza

PURSE

el bolso

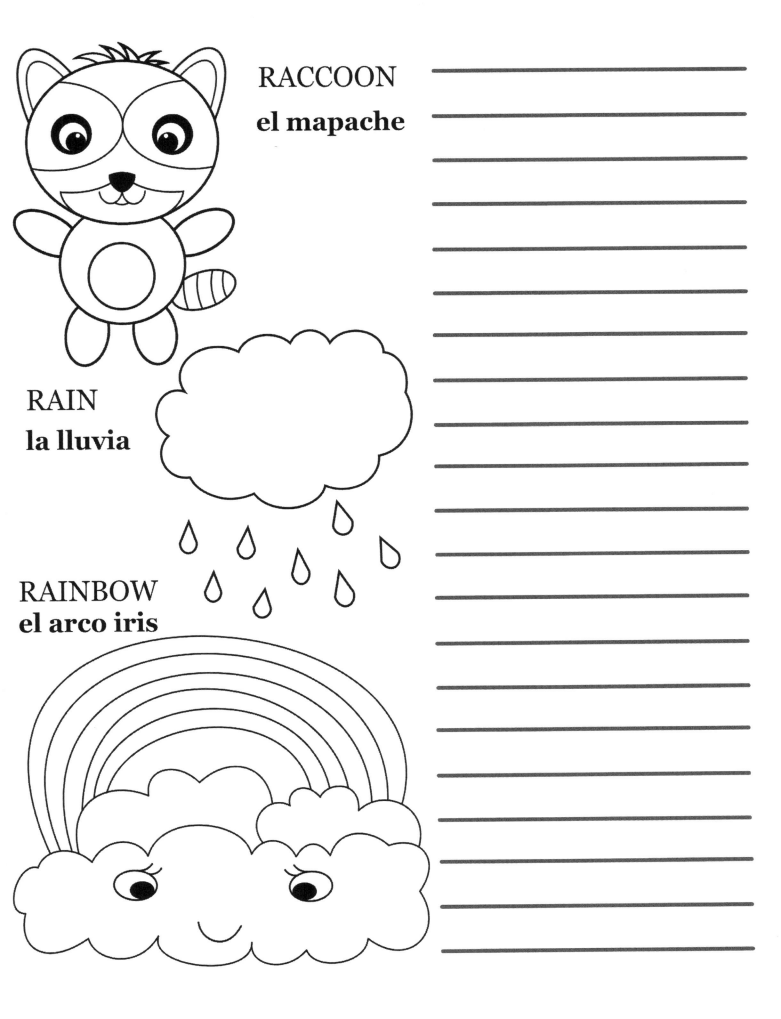

RACCOON
el mapache

RAIN
la lluvia

RAINBOW
el arco iris

RAM **el carnero**

RAT

la rata

RECORD

el disco

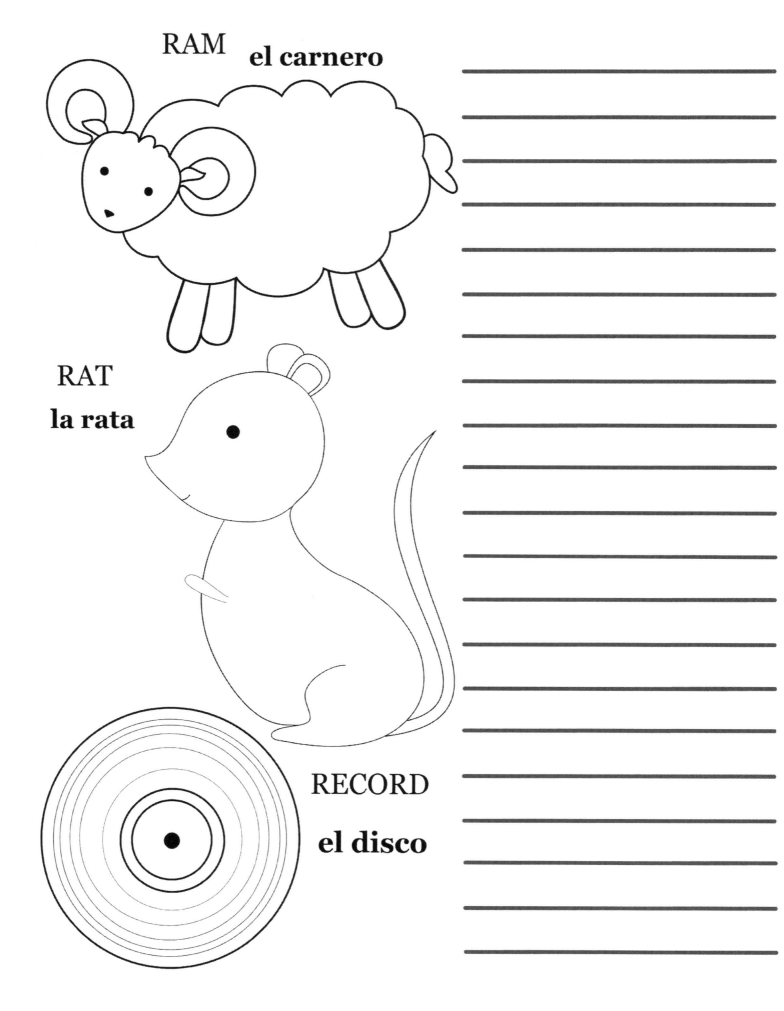

REINDEER
el reno

RHINOCEROS
el rinoceronte

RING
el anillo

ROCKET SHIP
el cohete espacial

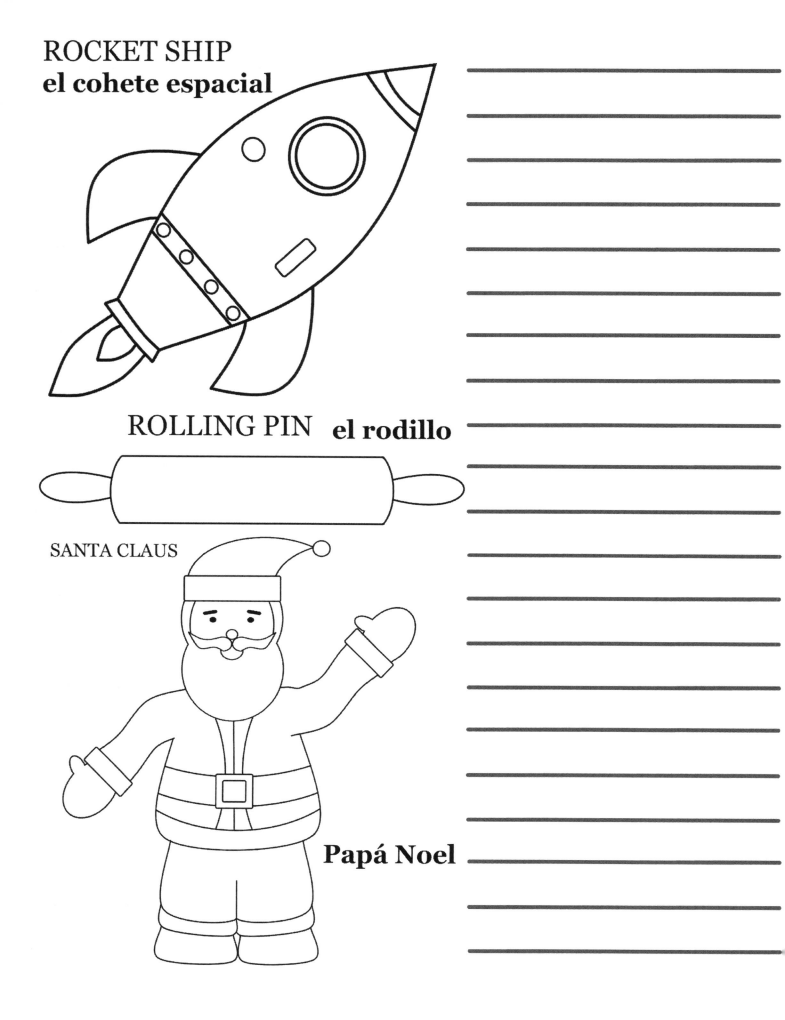

ROLLING PIN   **el rodillo**

SANTA CLAUS

Papá Noel

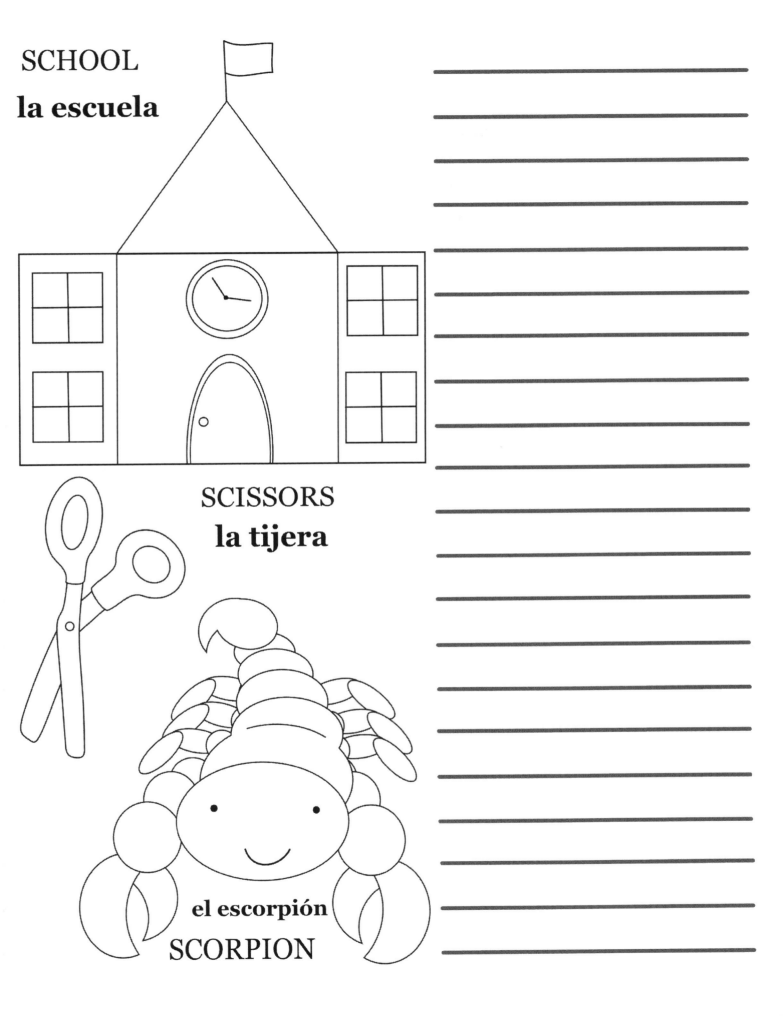

SCHOOL
la escuela

SCISSORS
la tijera

el escorpión
SCORPION

SEAHORSE

el caballito de mar

SHARK
el tiburón

SHEEP
la oveja

SHIP   **el barco**

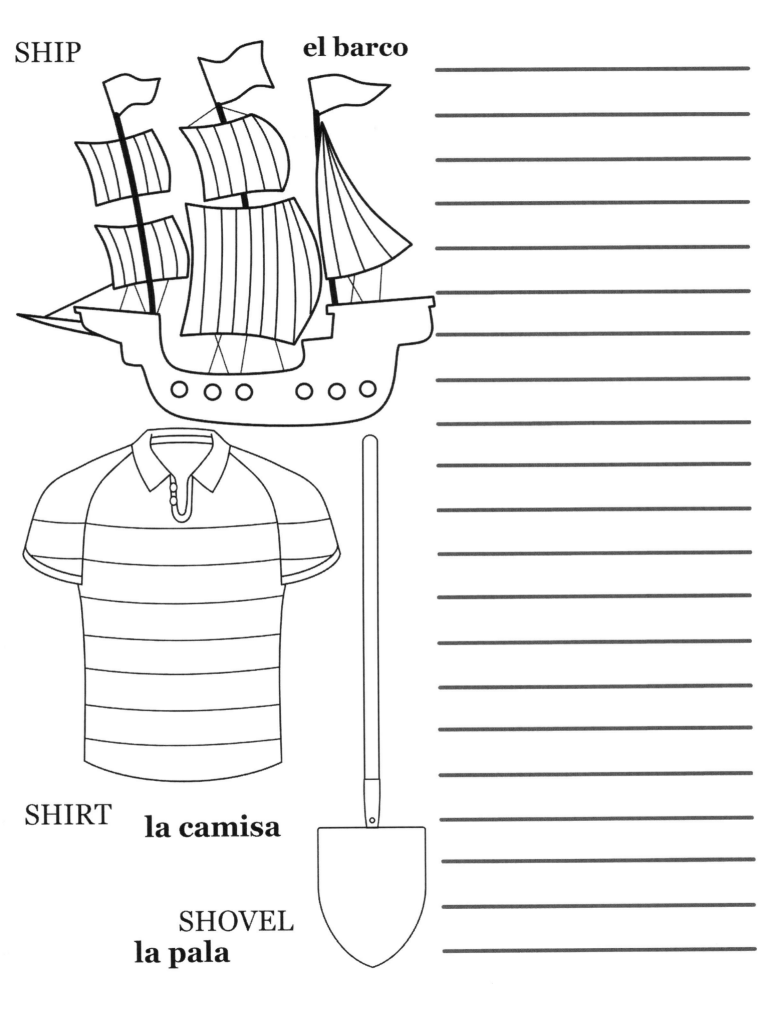

SHIRT   **la camisa**

SHOVEL
la pala

SISTER
la hermana

SKATE
el patín

SKATEBOARD
el monopatín

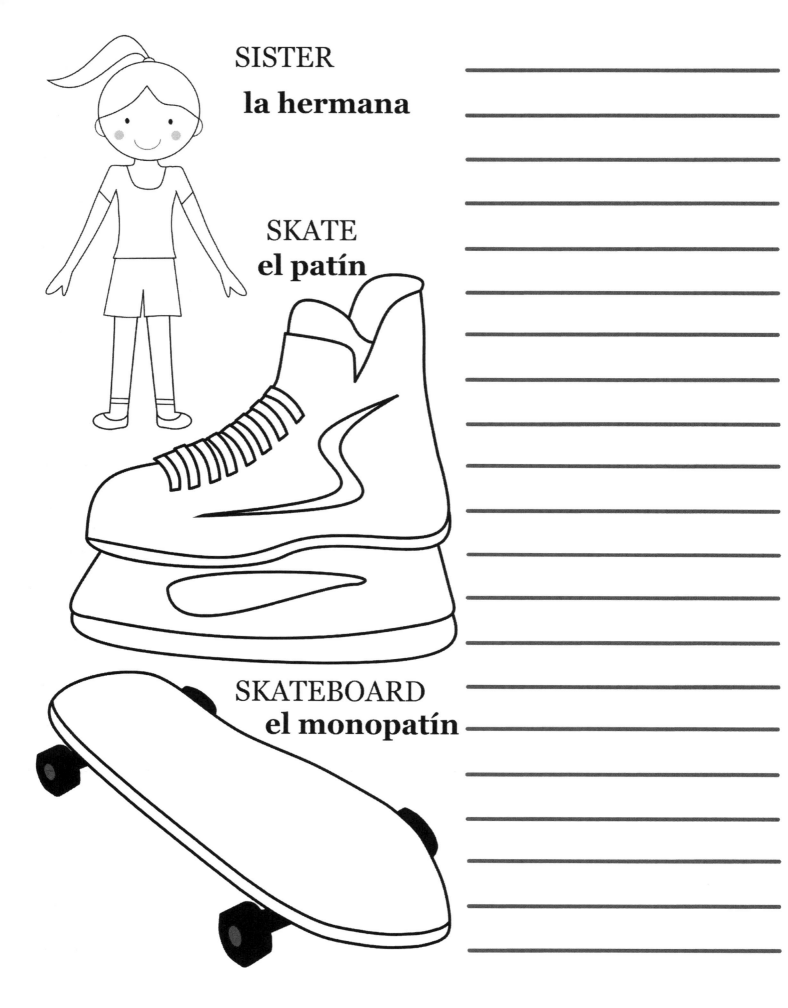

SKIRT
la falda

SKUNK
la mofeta

SKY

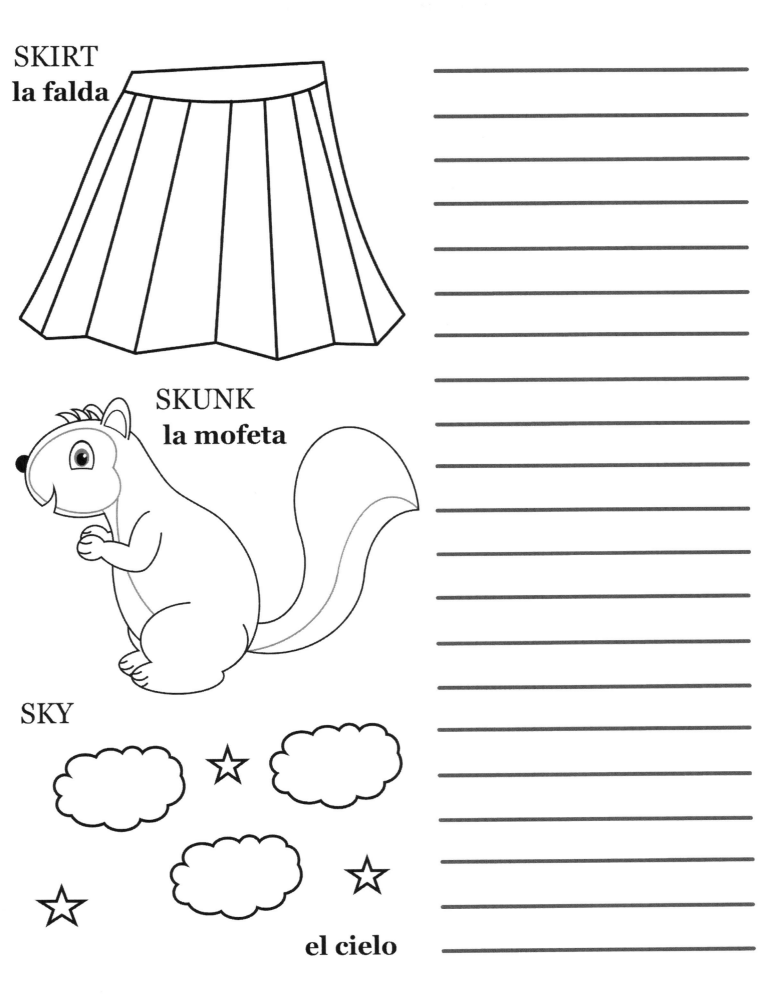

el cielo

SLOTH **el perezoso**

SNAIL
el caracol

SNAKE
la serpiente

SNOWFLAKE
el copo de nieve

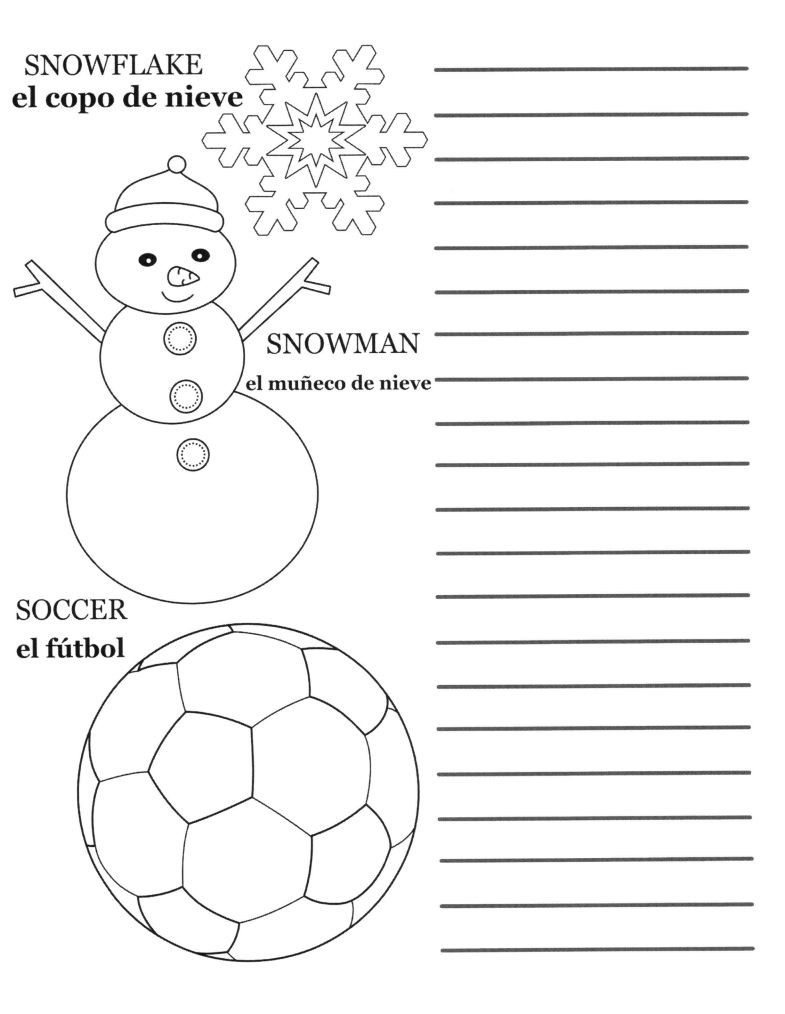

SNOWMAN

el muñeco de nieve

SOCCER
el fútbol

_____

_____

_____

_____

_____

_____

_____

_____

_____

_____

_____

_____

_____

_____

_____

_____

_____

_____

SPIDER **la araña**

SPOON

la cuchara

SQUID

el calamar

SQUIRREL **la ardilla**

STAR
la estrella

STINGRAY

la raya venenosa

STORK

la cigüeña

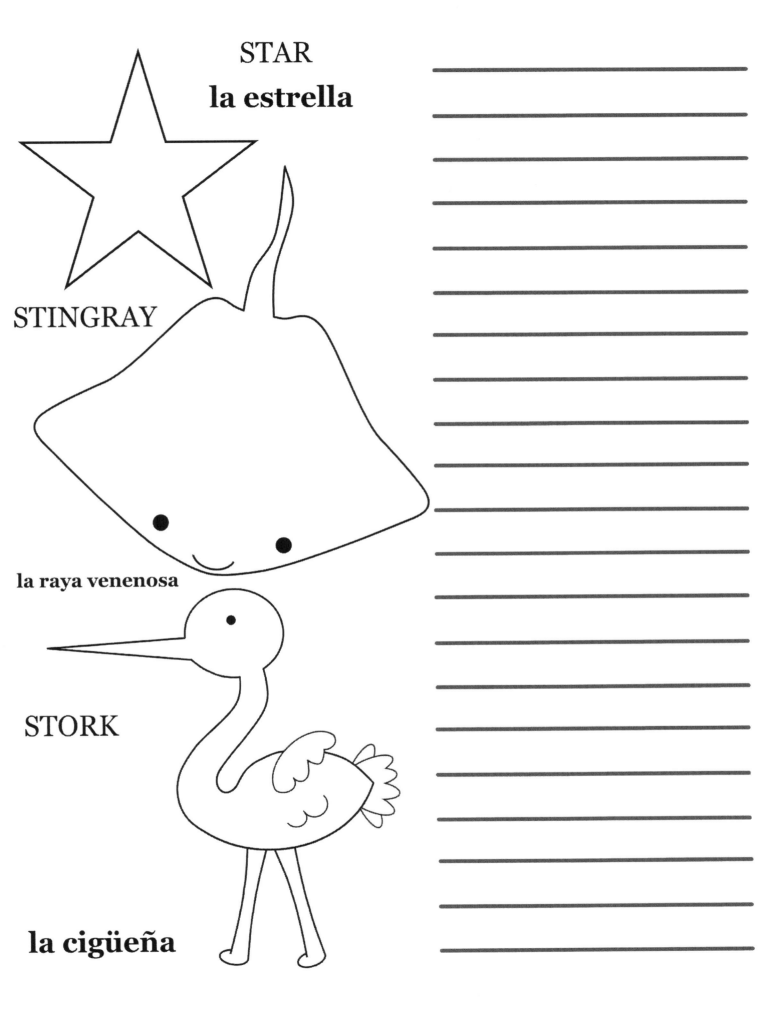

STOVE
la cocina

STRAWBERRY
la fresa

SUBMARINE
el submarino

LUGGAGE

el equipaje

SUN

el sol

SUNGLASSES

las gafas de sol

SWAN

el cisne

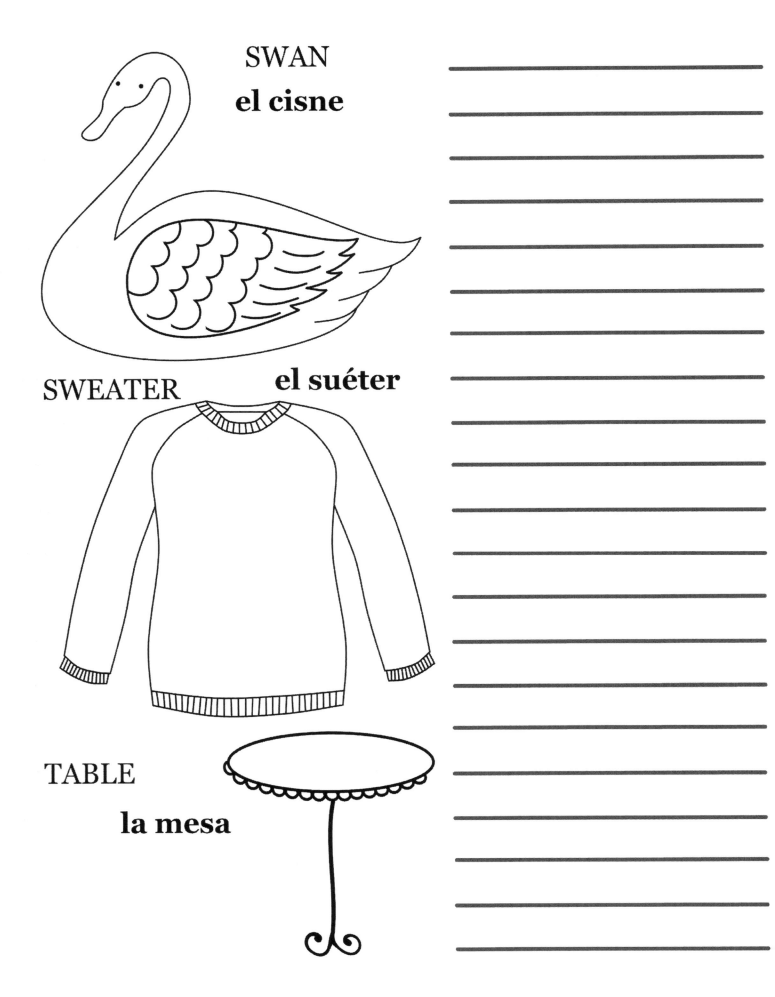

SWEATER   **el suéter**

TABLE

la mesa

TAXI   **el taxi**

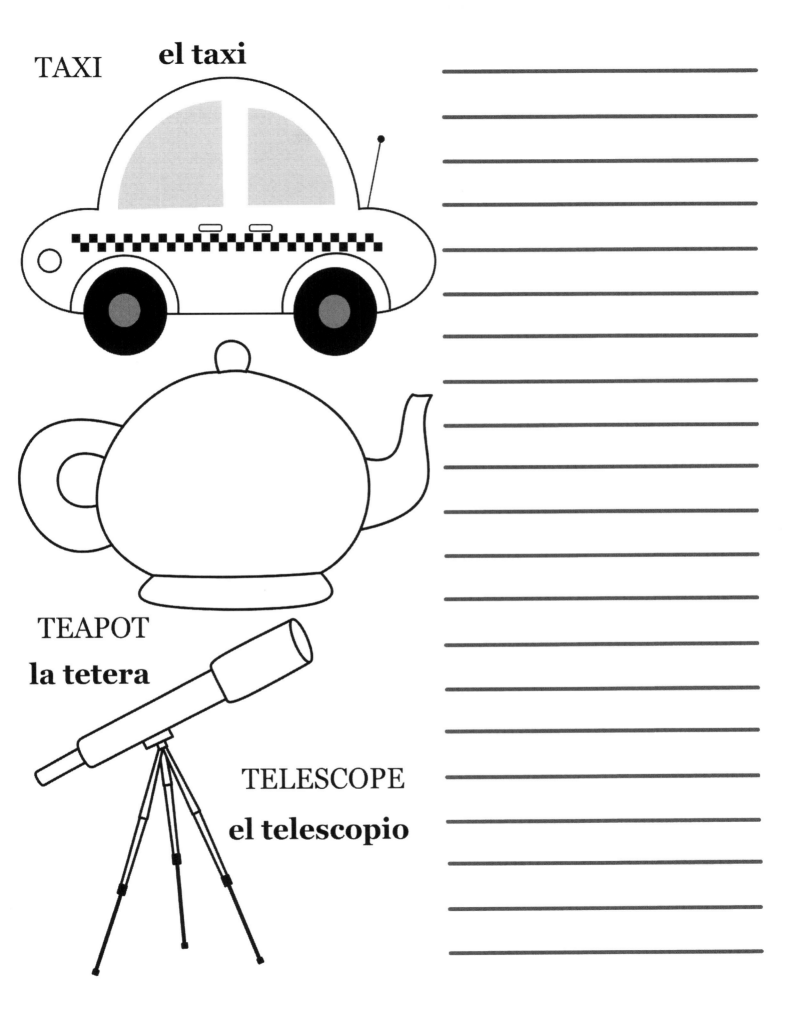

TEAPOT

la tetera

TELESCOPE

el telescopio

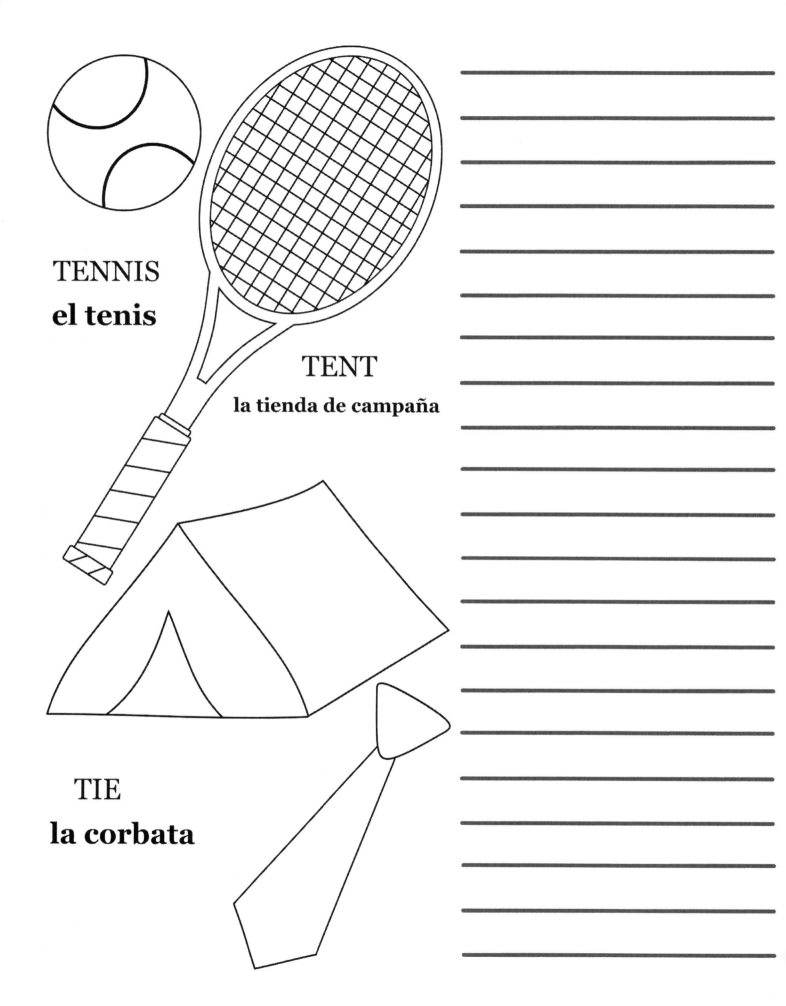

TENNIS
el tenis

TENT
la tienda de campaña

TIE
la corbata

TIGER

el tigre

TIPI

el tipi

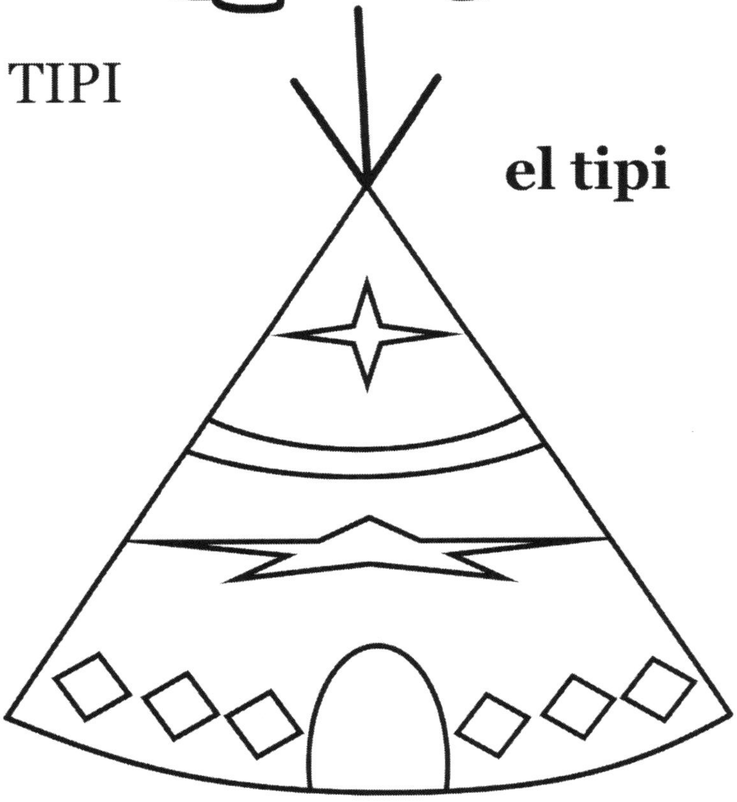

TOMATO
el tomate

TOOTH   el diente

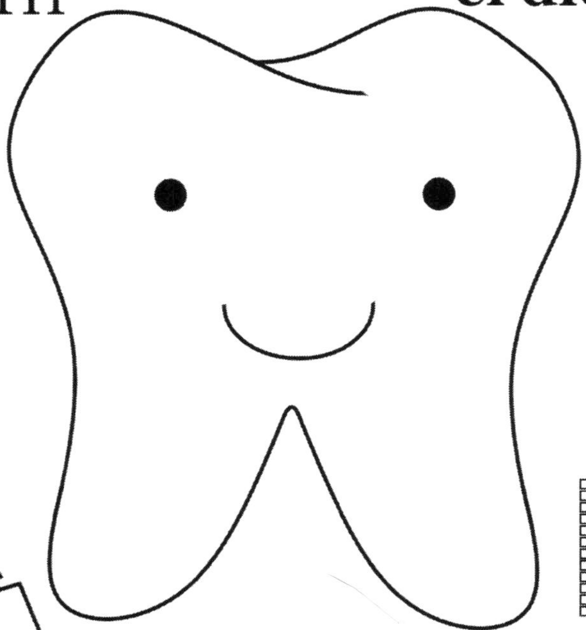

el dentífrico

TOOTHPASTE

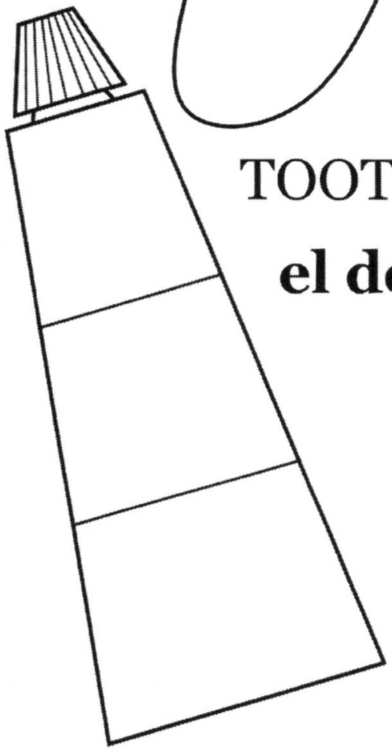

TOOTHBRUSH

el cepillo
de dientes

TRACTOR

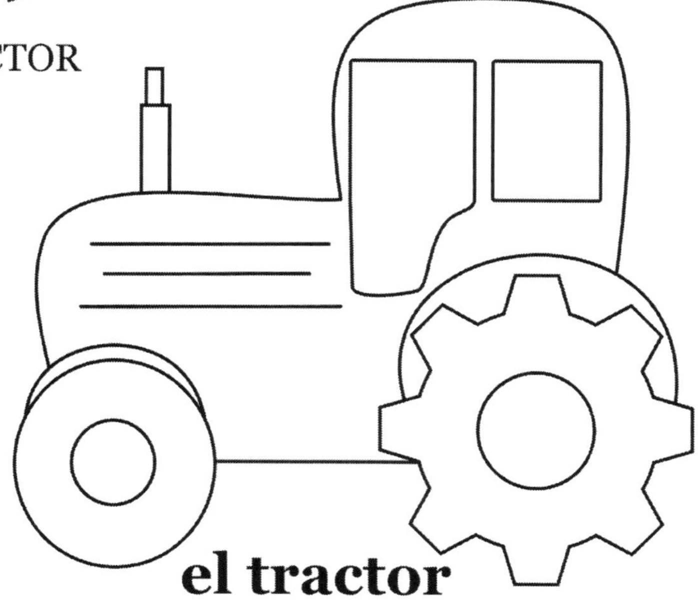

el tractor

TRAIN

el tren

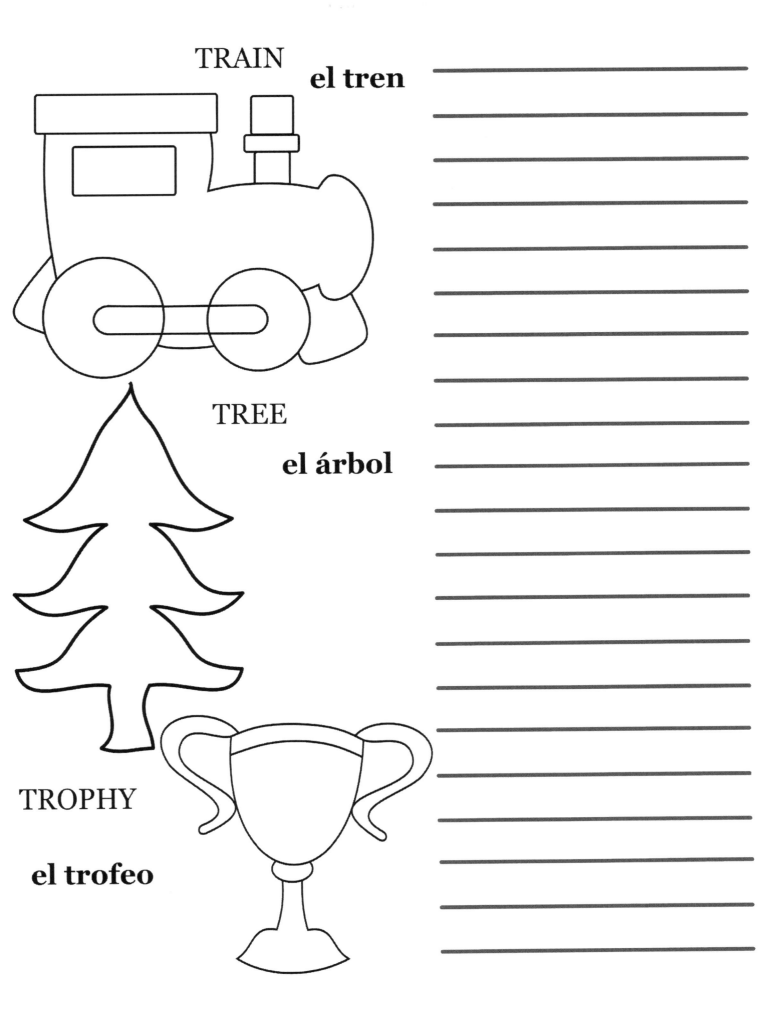

TREE

el árbol

TROPHY

el trofeo

TRUCK
el camión

TURKEY
el pavo

TURTLE

la tortuga

TELEVISION
el televisor

UMBRELLA **el paraguas**

UNICORN
el unicornio

el voleibol
VOLLEYBALL

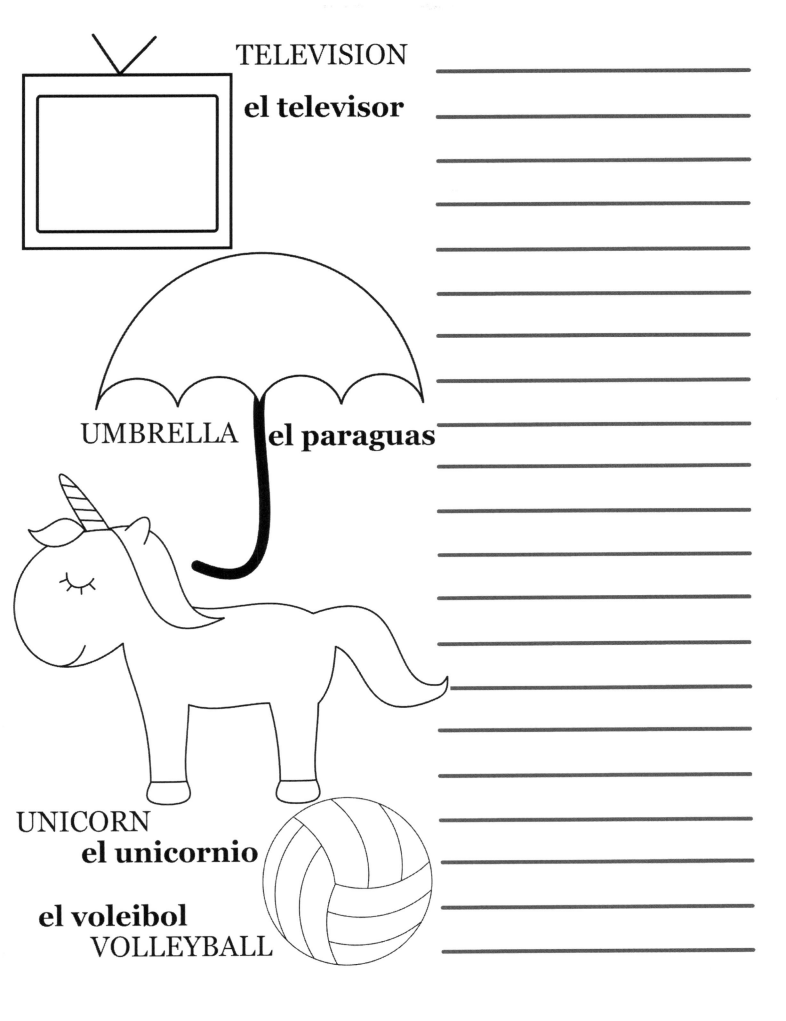

WALRUS
la morsa

WAND
la varita mágica

WATCH
el reloj

WATERMELON
la sandía

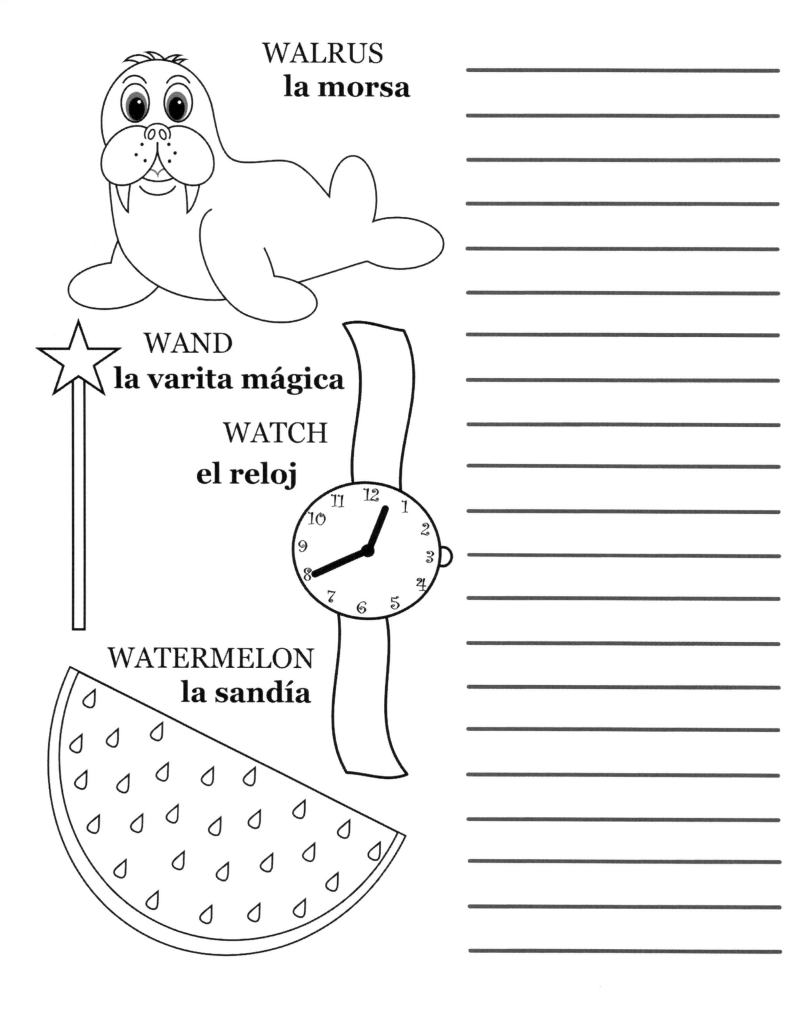

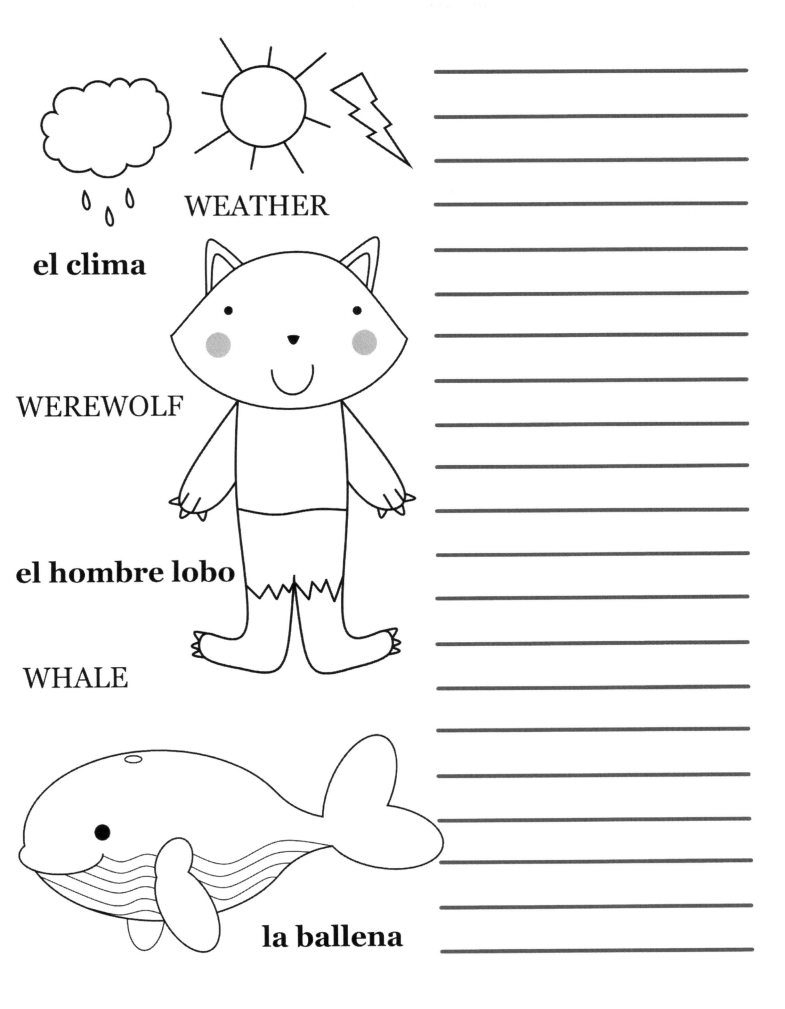

WEATHER

el clima

WEREWOLF

el hombre lobo

WHALE

la ballena

WITCH **la bruja**

WOLF **el lobo**

WORM
el gusano

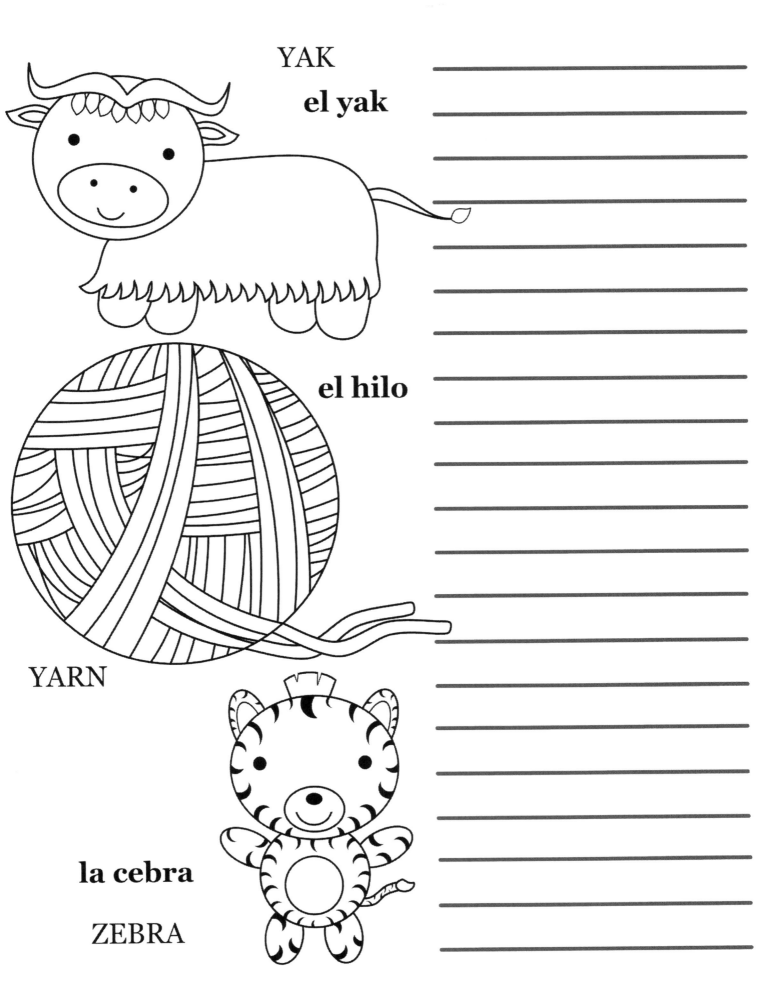

YAK

el yak

el hilo

YARN

la cebra

ZEBRA

SQUARE

el cuadrado

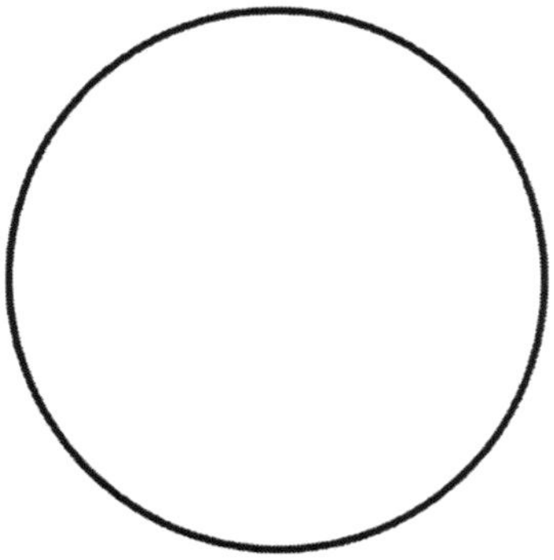

CIRCLE

el círculo

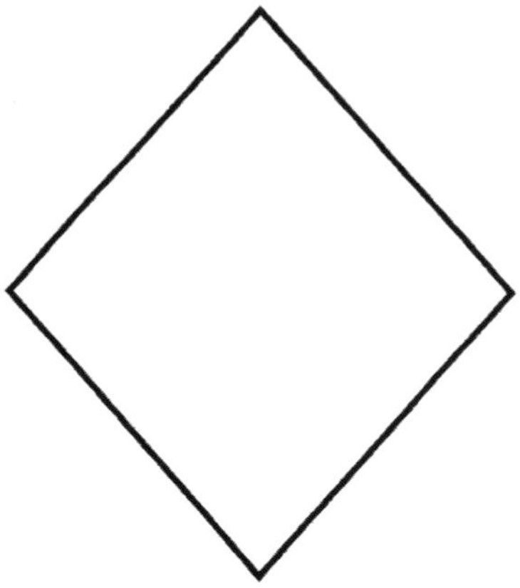

DIAMOND

el rombo

RECTANGLE

el rectángulo

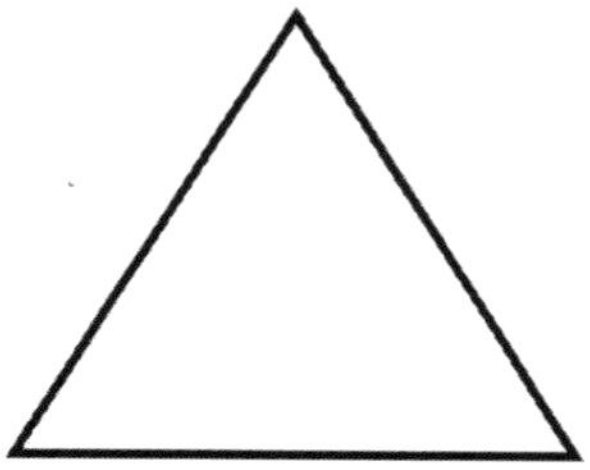

TRIANGLE

el triángulo

1 ONE un _____

_____

2 TWO dos _____

_____

3 THREE tres _____

_____

4 FOUR cuatro _____

_____

5 FIVE cinco _____

_____

6 SIX seis _____

_____

7 SEVEN siete _____

_____

8 EIGHT ocho _____

_____

9 NINE nueve _____

_____

10 TEN diez _____

_____

RED
el rojo

YELLOW
el amarillo

ORANGE
el naranja

PURPLE
el morado

GREEN
el verde

BLUE
el azul

WHITE
el blanco

BLACK
el negro

PINK
el rosado

Made in the USA
San Bernardino, CA
12 December 2019